VINTAGE BREADBOARDS

In memory of my mother, Rosslyn, who
started the collection that forms the basis of the
Antique Breadboard Museum.

VINTAGE BREADBOARDS

Madeleine Neave
with photos by Kourosh Monirzad
research by Tom Samuel
and recipes by Marie Lester

PROSPECT BOOKS

2019

First published in Great Britain and the United States in 2019 by Prospect Books, 26 Parke Road, London, SW13 9NG.

British Library Cataloguing in Publication Data:
A catalogue entry for this book is available from the British Library.

ISBN 978-1-909248-64-9

Printed and bound by Gutenberg Press Ltd., Malta.

Contents

The Staff of Life

As well as having an obsession for bread, I've also had an obsession for all things woody. My breadmaking efforts are mixed to say the least, ranging from the delicious to totally inedible jaw breakers – it's a science I have yet to master. My obsession for wood came from serving as a specialist in the European Works of Art department at Christie's for thirty years, where I developed a love of early domestic utensils, and in particular a love and passion for 'treen' (small domestic utensils, especially made of wood), its an old word meaning 'made of tree'.

Objects that have served a purpose over decades, and in some cases centuries, give me immense pleasure. A life of service leaves its marks, the wear and tear, a slight warp, a shrinkage crack or two, a multitude of little scratches, a depth of patina – all bear witness to their history. The fact that many of these objects still survive today, especially the humble breadboard, shows that they were also often treasured. I have several breadboards myself, one of which belonged to my late mum, and another which she inherited from her mum. I rarely use them these days but could never part with them.

You can imagine my delight when I discovered that there was actually a museum devoted to the humble breadboard in London. My first visit to the Antique Breadboard Museum was a revelation, just a little front room in a Putney cottage – but what a room! So many beautiful breadboards, carefully curated and amassed over the last four or five decades by the late Rosslyn Neave, and now taken over by her daughter Madeleine. It was a pleasure handling the collection and contributing my knowledge of early treen to Madeleine's book.

Sheaves of wheat and mottos abound in the carvings on the boards, but what is easy to overlook is the quality of the craftsmanship: if you've ever tried to carve a piece of wood you'd understand. Such simple but beautiful objects, mostly made from the humble sycamore tree; seeing them all together in this room created a feeling of warmth and hospitality. In an age of mass production where moulded plastic has infiltrated every aspect of our lives, they evoked a yearning to revert back to a simpler and more wholesome way of life.

Madeleine's beautiful book is the first to celebrate this endangered craft and tradition, and it serves as a lasting testament to her mother's collection.

Nic McElhatton
Chairman, Christie's South Kensington, 2010-17

1.

Introduction
by
Madeleine Neave

'Welcome', sycamore, 1920s, 12 inches.

An Alternative Breadboard Glossary

'Niche', 'Quirky', you will be thinking, and yet breadboards are becoming celebrated in a number of wholesome, comforting trends.

Reviving Craft. Making a breadboard is a way of affirming the dignity of the artist in a mechanised age. Mastering any art is admirable, and breadboards encompass several skills – if you consider they first need a forester to manage the tree, a sawyer to cut prime planks, a turner to select the wood and shape the object and a carver or pyrographer to decorate it. Then there's the complex series of cutler's skills needed to prepare the bread knives. The Heritage Craft Association, with Prince Charles as its president, is doing a great job of encouraging new professionals and amateurs into making.

Collecting. We are a nation of collectors, and it is my theory that every street has a fabulous collection of something, boxed up in the attic. Many visitors to our Antique Breadboard Museum in Putney are closet collectors, though it's now a vilified hobby, tarred with the 'hoarding' brush. They come to be amused and see what we have done. Some may even be inspired to create their own 'homeum'. Why not display the fruits of our obsessions in our own front rooms, do the research, and throw our houses open to the public? Don't give it to an old museum – make your own! Democratise our heritage! Keep it away from the academics! We need a Soapbox Museum for a start.

Redefining 'Museum'. Museums are often seen as boring because we receive a Victorian schoolroom experience there, referred to as the 'empty-bucket' method of teaching. In short, the ignorant child (visitor) passively absorbs, while the teacher (museum) provides an impersonal information dump. If museums were subject to Ofsted criteria for 'learning through engagement', most would be in Special Measures. In a push-pull, on-demand age, curated tours with personalised Q&As are a far more attractive way to learn.

Returning to Wood. The last manufacturer of the quintessential British breadboard was crowded out in 2002 by plastic and cheap imported chopping boards. But plastic is by no means an ideal substance, harbouring bacteria in the knife marks and absorbing food colours (not to mention contributing to the plastic mountains and plastic tides that are polluting our planet), while cheap imported boards are made of inadequately seasoned wood and consequently have a short shelf life. Hopefully the short-term and the unsustainable will soon no longer be an option.

Nostalgia. For some of us, the family breadboard is so intrinsic to home and care-giving that we hardly notice it. But sometimes it takes a personal loss or crisis to remind us. This is why they were handed down, as heirlooms, charged with memories of childhood. My mother Rosslyn was unusual in giving breadboards the time of day during a period when they were not valued. Michael, a museum visitor, was inspired to write a whole piece on why he took his mum's breadboard back to his flat after having to put her in a home, mentioning 'the extraordinary ordinariness' of them: the very thing he was losing as his mum succumbed to Alzheimer's.

Artisan Baking. The health benefits of wholemeal have been expounded since 1880 by Dr Allinson, and now new craft bakers and home bakers are returning to a more wholesome loaf. Less bread in terms of quantity but better bread in terms of quality is now the fashion, as we try to manage gluten and calories. And what better than a nice breadboard to present your baking on?

Exploring the Mundane. Personal items give a very poignant insight into our lives, while also taking us on meandering journeys through history, politics, economics, art and values. This book spotlights a hitherto unnoticed object, in the same spirit as the Official Mandela Exhibition, the acclaimed play *If Beale Street Could Talk,* and the latest *If Walls Could Talk* from Dr Lucy Worsley. If your breadboard could talk…

Victoriana. In the bicentennial year of Queen Victoria's birth, a mushrooming of books, films and TV series have been revisiting the age with a back-office angle, such as ITV's *Victoria* and Amazon's *Peterloo.* A Victorian invention, breadboards possibly owe their very existence to the political and economic conflicts which also sparked Peterloo.

Personalisation. Breadboards have always followed the prevailing tastes of the time. In the past, the tentacles of Empire and world trade set off fashions for Gothic, Renaissance, Moorish and Art Nouveau styles.

Clutter vs Experiences. We all face conflict when choosing a gift, since the social pressure to declutter is strong, which explains the trend towards gift-experiences. Airbnb Experiences is a great platform for finding a fun solution and we are proud to part of their offering. Ironically, the Antique Breadboard Museum ticks both boxes by offering an experience about clutter!

Shop Local. Our museum visitors come from as far afield as Los Angeles and New Zealand, but we also welcome locals who wish to treat their friends and relatives to a reunion with a difference. So we have become a specialty tea-room for Valentine's Day, Mother's Day, birthdays, anniversaries – any excuse really. And I am bumping into my visitors all over Putney!

Keeping Dementia at Home. Alzheimer's blights so many lives and the care industry is not always the best solution. We kept Rosslyn at home and set up the breadboard collection in her front room so she could stay connected and grounded to her past passions. She never tried running away from her own home, and passed away among her breadboards.

Boomerangers. Rip-off rents have grounded many millennials, but rather than seeing this as a tragedy, it has been an enrichment for our family. The museum has an

Feature wall in the gallery inspired by Katrin Cargill's interior,
Homes & Gardens, October 2009.

online presence thanks to our son who has trained me in 'Insta' etiquette ('Don't post too often…') and blog management ('Just tell the story…').

Post-cancer. As a two-time survivor, I made the mistake of clinging to pre-cancer reality as a means of 'conquering the illness'. This led to years of self-inflicted fatigue. Joan, a counsellor at the Breast Cancer Haven in Fulham put it very nicely: 'It's time to reinvent yourself.' Start with what your body needs – in my case it was a daily nap – and rebuild around that. And prepare to be amazed!

Bremain. At 83, Rosslyn voted Remain. She was always berating politicians who did not 'know their history'. 'We never learn' was her catchphrase, in response to Europe's cycle of war and peace over the last 2,000 years. So far the EU has kept the peace – and that was more important than any other consideration in her view. As a war child, she was haunted by her memories. In a particularly vivid one, she was bedded down in a Warrington cellar as the bombs dropped. She stayed awake anxiously in the blackness, hearing her mother knitting on the stairs, as her brothers slept, oblivious.

Breadboards and knives on Rosslyn's Portobello Market stall, 1996.

Welcome to Rosslyn's Collection

This collection is the result of a series of serendipitous accidents. By chance Rosslyn found a pretty 'Our Daily Bread' breadboard in the East End in the early 1980s. Club Row and Brick Lane were still bombed out slum dwellings, with buddleia eating away at the brickwork and colourful characters scratching a living in the semi-habitable houses. Mum tried haggling the owner down from £5, but the lady did not relent, so mum left it on the understanding that if it was there the next week, she could have it for £3. She kicked herself all week. She was jubilant to find it the following Sunday and snapped it up. Having scrubbed it down she sold it, and thus began the 'breadboard phase'. She gradually became the go-to dealer. As the British were shedding their old-fashioned round boards in favour of rectangular ones, so the Americans and French were hoovering them up. She shipped box loads to the US, and developed a loyal customer base around the world. Among dealers she was known as fair, with a network of runners across the country, earning the nickname 'The Breadboard Lady' or 'BB' for short.

Again, unintentionally, she found herself unable to part with one "stunner" after another. Breadboard stalagmites started accreting, and knives covered chairs in neat rows. This was the landscape of my childhood, combined with teetering mountains of antique chairs awaiting restoration. She was a caner and rusher of seats during the week. Thus she lived, with her 'two hats', namely antiques and restoration.

But what to do with the hoard? In the 1990s, I suggested she write a book about them, and Rosslyn – after some misgivings about driving prices up – threw herself into researching her collection. She had enormous fun travelling to libraries, museums and archives, and visiting curators who gave her privileged access to their treasure troves. Breadboards are a common item of tableware, but they have passed almost unnoticed in academic tomes and reference books, so much legwork was done for scant reward.

The collection remained unknown until an interior designer, Katrin Cargill, spotted her stall in Portobello Market and hand-picked sixteen items to create a feature wall for *Homes & Gardens* magazine in 2009. There was much interest, but as they were not for sale, prospective buyers were disappointed. Information was gradually amassing about the collection but, by sorry happenstance, Rosslyn became so incapacitated with Alzheimer's that I not only had to shut her business down, but take over her whole life, inch by painful inch, with mum fighting me all the way. Her immense love for me as a child sustained me through this turbulent period and guided my decision to move back into her home to care for her. This required major adaptations, refurbishment and uprooting my family.

Rosslyn's Anecdotes

Among more than twenty box-loads of books and papers Rosslyn left, I found mostly notes, reference books and photocopies. So these reminiscences are precious in that they are an attempt at 'writing the book'. I have typed up verbatim the handwritten stories of her most memorable encounters with clients over forty years of buying and selling. I found myself crying and laughing in turns (both out loud), reliving how she charmed the grumpy husband, exactly as she tells it:

'I have to say I have never really understood the chord that is struck (by breadboards) in so many varied people from all over the world. I wonder if the stories themselves will illuminate the reason. Where to start? With an English girl in her twenties, perhaps. She took a long time choosing (they all do so I won't repeat it), but finally departed happy. The next week she returned to say she had bought it for her new flat – the only other piece of furniture she had was a bed – and that when her mother visited she was glad to see the breadboard and said she was settling down at last!

'A young man took ages and ages deciding which to go for, ranging the boards along the floor. It was for a wedding present he said. He then went through the process again in the choice of knife to accompany it. He spent some £70 which seemed a lot at the time and off he went. Next week he reappeared and my heart sank, imagining he had left them in a taxi or lost them somewhere. "No," he said, "I couldn't bear to give them away, so I've come back to buy another set."

'An American woman was aghast when, years ago, she was informed she would have to pay £25 for a board with 'Give Us This Day Our Daily Bread' around the edge. She said, what would her husband say if she told him what she'd paid? I said "Why tell him?" Next year she reappeared: "You remember that board for £25. Where is it?" But she departed empty-handed, cross with herself for having missed the opportunity of buying it the previous year.

'A charming young Italian who, I later discovered, was a lawyer working on his degree in London, longed for a knife and board, but his budget was tight and after a good deal of huffing and puffing I recommended he choose one or the other. But which? (It is annoying to split them when you find a good match). I suggested finally that he settle for the knife (which is harder to find) and when he became a rich and successful lawyer to be sure to return for a board.

'An American couple in their fifties or sixties arrived, and the wife exclaimed, "Oh darling, I've always wanted one of these!" "What would you do with it?" he replied. "Serve cheese and ham and cut bread." "Well, I'm not carrying it." He stood in the middle of the room. His wife searched gingerly in the boxes and I asked him why he was so grouchy. "I'm feeling cold." "No wonder," I said, "you're not dressed correctly." He had a coat and jacket and scarf on, but they were unbuttoned and the scarf was just hanging uselessly. So I took the scarf off, pulled the coat back, did up the jacket buttons, tied the scarf and did up the buttons of the coat. Meanwhile, the wife had gone through the boxes, selected two and said, "Darling, which do you like best?" And he said, "Whichever you prefer, I leave it to you". I wondered what memories of Portobello Road they would have every time it was put on the table.

'A couple from New Zealand, maybe sixty-five or so, quiet, civilised, examined the boards. "We want one for a special occasion." The wife explained that her husband, a surgeon, was visiting a patient of his on a Greek Island (I kick myself for not asking which one) who had been terribly ill. They chose a board with a Biblical motto, and after a memorable and quiet encounter, they departed happily. Next year they returned. They had visited the patient and the husband had wondered when the correct moment to give his present would occur, when the lady asked them if they would like to go to her chapel. He excused himself for a moment and went upstairs to his luggage, returning with the board. In the chapel he gave it to her and she was so touched she put it on the altar and it was blessed. It stays there. The second visit was to buy a knife to go with the board.

'A couple, maybe a mother and her son, who was particularly caring in a distant sort of way. He stood in awe perhaps, but she needed looking after. She might have been older than she looked. He looked fifty or so. She was interested in the boards and the selection process started. Choice is difficult when there are nearly a hundred, with a wide range of prices. She picked out several with mottos, and plain ones, but they suddenly found themselves surrounded by a crowd whose selection process was easier and so the couple departed quietly saying they'd return. Which they did, to somewhat depleted supplies, making it easier to focus. The crowd had stirred up the boxes, bringing to the surface one the woman had missed first time around. It was a board I've only ever seen once, with a very wide, incised border, maybe 2 ½ inches deep, incorporating the symbolic wheat and leaves and a simplified crucifix. She picked it up slowly. "I am a Minister. I will take that board." The centre was minute, just a couple of inches across. "It'll accommodate the Host."

'My daughter went to Bremen to continue the German course she had started at the Goethe Institute in London. A family on our square told her to look up friends of theirs in Bremen. They also had two houses in Switzerland, one for them to live in and the other for their collection of dolls. Interesting people, my daughter thought! Dinner invitation followed. Bread and cheese was served at the end, and on the board was a knife with "Bread" carved on the handle. Madeleine quietly examined it. "I bought it in London," her hostess explained. Madeleine asked where. "Well, there was a woman at the top of Portobello…" "With curly hair?" Madeleine interrupted. "Why yes," was the astonished reply. "That came from my mother!"'

Madeleine's Museum

Again, what to do with the hoard of breadboards? The Alzheimer's Society's advice to keep Rosslyn connected with her past was a crucial factor in spurring me on to turn our front room into a gallery, hung with her breadboards and knives. Displayed in creative ways which were both attractive and safe, she could keep in touch with her old passion in what became her therapy room, where she sat for hours polishing, shuffling and hiding her most cherished pieces.

The museum welcomed the general public for the first time during the Wandsworth Arts Fringe 2017, attracting a handful of local visitors, who were given a guided tour and cream tea, with Rosslyn holding court where possible. The hands-on approach, combined with enjoying the breadboards in their original context, made the experience more personal and meaningful.

And the information flowed both ways. As silent companions at the heart of most kitchens and dining rooms, breadboards have been triggering intimate memories among guests, memories that are often shared in the trusting, warm atmosphere created by a generous cream tea! With permission, I have harvested these anecdotes and presented them on the blog in the Visitors' Book which has inadvertently become a social history archive, as I am careful to ascertain the location and decade of each story. A choice selection of these insights on how people actually used their breadboards can be found in the Top Tips section.

After Rosslyn passed away, and all the ghastly paperwork was completed, the hoard again awaited my decision: box it all up and auction it off? Rosslyn had always joked about throwing her home open to the public, as guests used to stare goggle-eyed at her Victorian knick-knacks. I thought: why not? It has become my personal response to her life and death, a form of grief therapy which celebrates her forty years of collecting and her love for me.

Museum Tour FAQs

The tours have been running almost weekly – and sometimes daily – since December 2017. Mostly guests arrive fizzing with questions, so here follows a selection:

What are these?! (Asked by those who have been given a surprise gift-experience!) You take your plain wooden chopping board and you market it as being exclusively for cutting and presenting bread. You make it pretty. But everyone's idea of pretty is different, as is their budget, so you cater.

Are they round because trees are round?

Breadboards are made from planks cut along the trunk, so they all start off square. We think they are round because the early carvers were mimicking the shape of traditional serving platters. And bread was mostly round before baking tins.

How old is your oldest?

The earliest board in Rosslyn's collection dates from 1848 and was made by a carver called Mr Rogers in Soho, London.

How long have they been around?

Impossible to say, since we have not found evidence proclaiming the 'first ever' breadboard. We know they were being produced in the late 1820s at least.

Why all this effort for, essentially, a chopping board?

We have a theory. Breadboards began, we think, when bread was very expensive, during the Corn Law period. Carvers saw an opportunity to sell decorative items to display what had become a precious commodity. When wheat prices were slashed and bread became affordable again, everybody wanted a breadboard to celebrate.

Do the patterns have meaning?

A wheat motif signifies the board was for bread because wheat was the cereal of choice for bread in the South. During the period of the Corn Laws, a wheat motif on your board probably meant you supported Richard Cobden – an activist trying to get the Corn Laws repealed. Wheat also has symbolic connections, with the Christian religion and Holy Communion, and in Roman times it was also the symbol of Ceres, the goddess of harvest and fertility.

How many visitors so far?

About 350, as of July 2019.

What do you enjoy most?

I love hearing breadboard stories. They are so personal and often very funny. And I get excited when a guest unlocks a mystery in the collection. People know so much and always contribute something interesting.

What do you think of it all?

Creating her gallery and pulling the research together has been a painful but fulfilling process. I grew up around the boards, witnessing mum's joy after a buying trip. Every board was hard-earned, every profit margin negotiated. I've read through every page of research, conducted tours for nearly two years, and feel that, whether I like it or not, I am the best person to commit her story and breadboard history to paper. But none of it could have happened without the team and a galaxy of kind individuals who gave up their time and know-how (see the 'Acknowledgements' section).

2.

TOP TIPS

Caring For Your Board

Cleaning. Boards that are in use should be washed with warm water using a washing-up pad, and dried thoroughly before being left to air. Ensure the board is totally dry before putting it away, or it might warp. Letting it sit in its own puddle by the draining board rots the wood over time. Dishwashers destroy boards. Also be careful not to leave them on the hob in case they get scorched by residual heat. Store them away from the hob, or the heat will dry them out and split them.

Steady conditions. Boards are most prone to splitting if there are sudden changes in temperature and humidity, so keeping these constant, or ensuring a gradual change over some days, will help to keep the wood intact. Dropping them shouldn't split them.

Nourishing. If the board is looking bleached or pale, it is too dry. Use kitchen paper to apply a sparing coat of Rustins Worktop Oil, which is food-safe. Vegetable oils such as sunflower, linseed, or olive oil are also effective, although

A cracked sycamore board mended by screwing a thin board onto the reverse.

make sure you choose one with a smell you like. Use the board as usual, but leave it out and standing up to dry over several days. It will feel oily for some weeks, but the oil will soak in and nourish the wood, providing a protective, waterproof film. The grain will also look rich and colourful. Repeat this process depending on frequency of use.

Sanding. Wooden boards are more hygienic than plastic because wood absorbs whatever is on the surface, like our skin, so bacteria sink down under the surface, reducing the risk of cross-contamination. Periodically, you need to lightly sand the cutting surface away, to remove any bacteria that has not been killed by the wood's natural anti-bacterial properties.

Waxing. Display boards can have a thin coat of wax to feed them very occasionally. This should be followed by a lot of rubbing with a soft cloth. It is the rubbing that gives the sheen, too much wax will just make them sticky. The wax should be natural wax, not silicone or aerosol.

Recarving. Jeff got in touch looking for a wood carver to take things one step further. He wants to undo the ravages of time – he is proposing to scoop it up from his late father's house and have it re-carved to restore its former appearance.

Jeff's family board used every day for at least 50 years.

Choosing a Breadboard

A successful breadboard is the result of hundreds of invisible decisions by the turner and carver – though these are not the subject of this book. We are probably more familiar with those less successful boards made of three or four strips of poorly-seasoned wood that last 5-10 years before warping and splitting. They are mostly thrown away or demoted to the man-shed or log-pile. The benefit is they are relatively cheap (£10-20) and are a convenient quick fix.

Anne's wedding board in three pieces, still in use after 40 years!

Keepsake. While buying more durable wooden boards would reduce plastic and waste, there is a much more deep-seated reason for buying a future 'heirloom': it becomes a precious keepsake of a departed loved one. John moved back into his mum's home after she passed away. 'Did the board get culled?' I asked, to which he answered, astonished at the thought, 'No, it's far too precious!' At the end of the tour, he said he was going home to give it a hug!

One piece of wood. A durable board has certain features. First and foremost, it must be made of one piece of wood, because wood continues to behave like living skin when sawn. It responds constantly to humidity and heat, respecting the old pulls of the mother tree. But it can't be from any old bit of a tree.

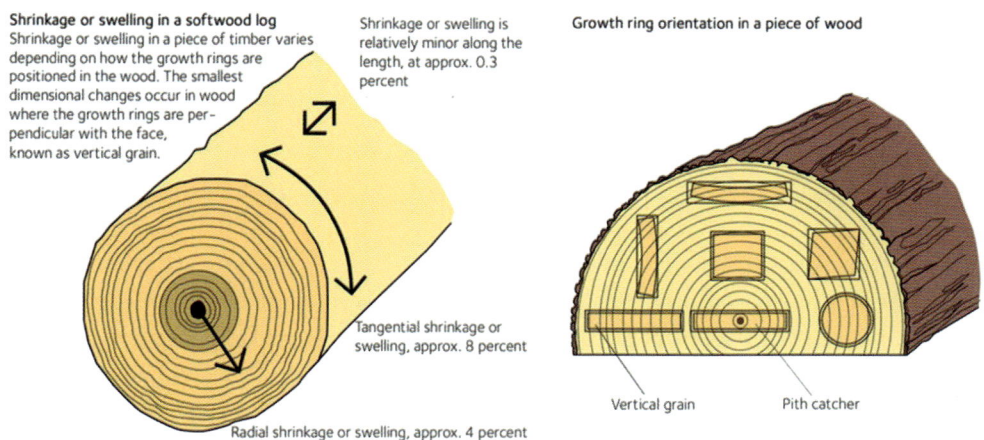

Shrinkage or swelling in a softwood log
Shrinkage or swelling in a piece of timber varies depending on how the growth rings are positioned in the wood. The smallest dimensional changes occur in wood where the growth rings are per-pendicular with the face, known as vertical grain.

Shrinkage or swelling is relatively minor along the length, at approx. 0.3 percent

Growth ring orientation in a piece of wood

Tangential shrinkage or swelling, approx. 8 percent

Radial shrinkage or swelling, approx. 4 percent

Vertical grain   Pith catcher

Showing three-way shrinkage across a trunk. Courtesy of Swedish Wood.

Choice cuts. The diagram shows how wood shrinks and swells along three axes, causing the shape to morph. The choicest cuts are 'quartersawn' (labelled 'vertical grain' in the diagram), because the arrangement of the grain is in parallel lines and means the shape will not be deformed by shrinkage, it will remain flat and simply become slightly oval. The cheap 'flat' and 'rift' sawn cuts lead to warping and will eventually make the board unusable.

If you align two bits of wood from different parts of a tree, or from different trees, they will shrink or swell in their own directions radially (across the growth rings), tangentially (along the growth rings), and longitudinally (along the trunk). Also, the glue will degrade over time, becoming less efficient at keeping the jostling strips or blocks of wood aligned. Mosaic boards are very attractive, in the style of miniature butchers' blocks, but again the more joins there are the weaker the product becomes.

Optimum weight. This is an important factor, determining whether the board will be a pleasure to use or too cumbersome. Weight is allied to wood type and thickness, and the optimum thickness is about an inch, as anything less will compromise its strength.

Choice of wood This should be informed not only by its hues and patterns, but also by its suitability for food preparation. Medium-hard to hard is the most desirable, as well as a tight grain in order to prevent water being absorbed too easily and food residue getting caught. British breadboard makers mostly used sycamore, but there are many exotic alternatives today.

Uses For a Breadboard

Since the Antique Breadboard Museum opened, I have had the pleasure of meeting many visitors and hearing their reminiscences about bread and breadboards. What started as a personal record of each visit for future guests to enjoy, grew into a social history archive. Breadboards were so central to daily routines that many anecdotes shine a very intimate light on family dynamics. There follows a selection of stories about the numerous possible uses of a breadboard, all gathered from our guests or Rosslyn's family. It is heartening to hear how breadboards are still a quietly indispensable item in our kitchen landscape.

The Anti-Sliced. It is often thought that sliced bread was the death knell for the breadboard, but a few anecdotes disprove this theory. Clearly the country was divided. Diane complained bitterly to her mother about her buying pre-sliced bread in the late 1940s and early 50s, and Avril's friend's father wouldn't have it in the house.

Showing off your baking. Starting with the obvious – breadboards are great for celebrating home bakers. For example, Nic loved baking but his kitchen skills

Nic's new board, its leaves possibly inspired from designs by Adam, who was in turn inspired by Classical art and architecture. Sycamore, 1900s, 12 inches.

had taken a back seat due to having to earn a living. He was inspired by his newly-acquired board to make some bread again, and was so chuffed with the result that he posted his achievement on his Instagram account (@way_side_boy) as proof!

Showing respect. A more subtle use maybe, but one that sticks in my mind. Gran used to ask me at tea if I wanted 'Crust or crumb?' Her simple question must have been very meaningful for me to have held on to it. Looking back, it probably stems from a sense of privilege at being given a choice which was respected, and getting first dibs. Rosslyn had an everyday breadboard (in addition to the collection) which we still use as our family board, but I have no image of her cutting bread for me, so she can't have involved me in the operation. In another flashback, I can still feel the joy of pinching away at the crust of a warm 'large white bloomer' in the back of our beige VW Variant, while mum popped into the laundromat. Maybe 'Crust' was never an option because I had already nibbled it off!

Mint sauce making. Ann's mum used the breadboard to prepare mint sauce, so for Ann, 'breadboard' says 'Sunday Roast'. Mum had a special wheely cutter, running it back and forth vigorously over the leaves, then scraping them back together before having another go. The wonderful smell of mint filled the kitchen, combined with a touch of vinegar which puddled in the central dip!

Tenderising ormers. Barbara had a flashback about the day her mother's breadboard split in two. Her mother was tenderising an ormer (abalone), a delicacy in Guernsey where she grew up. 'There are only four "ormering tides" in a year for collecting them, and you are only allowed to shore-gather the shellfish (no diving). When you have scraped it off the rock, you have to put the rock back exactly as you found it.' Fascinating!

Presenting cheese. Margaret and Richard brought their wedding board (1967) all the way from Romford. 'We flick it over for cheese. We have moved five times and it is always the last thing to pack and the first to unpack!' It's worth noting that rectangular bread from baking tins came in with the Industrial Revolution (1840s) and commercialised bakeries. Maureen observed that tins made the loaves swell up instead of out, fitting more in the ovens. Bread also became stackable. But rectangular boards like Margaret's only came in after the First World War, suggesting we have quite a conservative streak when it comes to food and tableware.

Double-sided. For others, the board was used on both sides, whether in the kitchen or on the dining table. Rosslyn's mother died in the 1970s so her father suddenly had to learn to cook, after a lifetime of not even needing to know where the sugar was kept. When using his kitchen one day, he made sure I was aware the board had an 'onion' side and an 'everything else' side.

Buttering. In families that moved to sliced bread, the board repositioned itself. Mike's parents' board was simple with a groove, and when sliced bread came in, it lived near the toaster and was used for buttering the toast. Similarly, Jan Higginson rang to say she was very glad to hear about our museum as she had her parents' breadboard sitting by the front door for months, waiting for her to find a moment to go to the local dump, and would we like it? 'I don't want it because it smells of rancid butter.' Her father used to butter his toast on it and didn't clean it properly. Using it in this way certainly had advantages though. Wood is far preferable to porcelain for keeping slices of toast warm, as wood's natural warmth absorbs less heat. Also, it absorbs the steam so the slices don't go limp.

Drinks tray. Jennifer used her board as an impromptu tray to serve drinks at her Wandsworth Artists Open House 2018 event. She is a consummate patchworker, and maker of all things textilian.

Bramhall board, 1930s-50s, sycamore, 12 inches. Courtesy of Jennifer Hollingdale.

Crushing meds. But boards aren't just used for food preparation. When the ambulance man came to help Rosslyn during a nasty chest infection, he offered some antibiotics in pill form.

'Just crush them up so she doesn't choke on them. Have you got a breadboard?' Our favourite Irish carer, Jeanette, looked at him wide-eyed and mirthful: 'Are you having a laugh? Didn't you see downstairs?'

Potstand. Another interesting question is where the board was kept. Rose's board stays in the kitchen and is nondescript; Marion's comes to the table and doubles as a potstand; Mary's grandmother's board had a bit of carving and stayed on the table, as there was no kitchen as such, just a sink, pantry, walk-in cupboard and a kitchen cabinet with a flap that became a work bench.

Getting arty. Frances got creative after she came to the museum with her husband Peter and two besties to celebrate his birthday. The whole day was masterminded by their daughters and they had NO idea what was in store. They were following a trail of crumbs in a series of envelopes. She made a breadboard collage to commemorate the day.

Wonderful Round Slice of Life for Pups 82nd Birthday 2018
by Frances Cowper Holzhausen Des RCA DMS. Courtesy of the artist.

Paint it. Michael Taylor RA, the well-known artist, particularly appreciated painting his mother-in-law's board and has incorporated it into his compositions no less than nine times. He explained how the dynamic circularity formed an eye-catching platform for his assemblages of domesticity, and a foreground for his very distinctive portraiture. We have a 'wing' devoted to his work, in miniature, in the museum.

Bread and Water, by Michael Taylor, RP, 1994. Courtesy of the artist.

Janice Hendra, an American artist, immortalised her breadboard in a dreamy, autobiographical watercolour depicting her kitchen. She bought the board in London in the 1970s and it, and the accompanying knife, has been with her ever since.

Kitchen Kit, watercolour by Janice Hendra. Courtesy of the artist.

Sculpt with it. Boards often come with a knife, but Daisy's bread knife sculpture has a more hard-hitting message. Her blood-drenched English bread knife was made for the French market, as the French word for 'bread' is 'pain'.

'The bread knife was bought during a trip to a brocante in France. I didn't make the assemblage until much later when I was going through a painful separation. Some love it and others hate it. Now it hangs on my kitchen wall as a reminder that pain in life is unavoidable but is also important as we grow and create through it and beyond it.'

Pain by artist Daisy Fior, 1980s. Courtesy of the artist.

Bequeath one. Jean called from her care home in Totnes in December 2017, to say she had a Mouseman breadboard which she was leaving in her Will to her friend 'who will appreciate it'. It is wonderful to hear that the board is so precious as to be given a special mention amongst all her chattels. A board can be a message of friendship even from beyond the grave.

Make one! Jane Dorner took it one step further and made her own personalised breadboards as gifts to celebrate the family relationships in her life, such as the one below for her mother, Lotte.

'Lotte', an oval board made of sycamore. Courtesy of Jane Dorner.

Collecting Antique Boards

Here are some guidelines for the novice collector from Sue Witts of Appleby Antiques.

Is it warped, scorched, chipped, cracked or worn beyond recognition?
Although many find such imperfections endearing, enhancing the 'character' and giving an insight into the story behind the board, you should be paying only half the going rate. The going rate is anything between £10 for a small worn board from the 1970s with square lettering, to hundreds of pounds for a rare specimen, depending on all the factors stated below.

How big is it?
Size can sometimes help with dating. Early Victorian boards were different sizes, but by the 1880s, they had become a standardised 12 inches. By the early 1900s, bread-platters were evolving into 'bread plates' 8-10 inches across, which could slot into a plate rack. But there are always exceptions and diameters sometimes reached 16 inches, depending on how deep the customer's pockets were, as bigger boards came from older, rarer trees.

What is the grain like?
A quality breadboard should be sourced from the choice cuts of a tree, that's to say the central planks running along the trunk, on either side of the centre. The annular rings should appear parallel and can be attractive with curve and wave formations. Knots, the stubs of branches where they join the tree, cause much wastage among quality makers as they will eventually fall out and leave a hole, compromising the durability of the wood. A board with a knot would have been sold cheaply as a 'second'.

What is the carving like?
In this brief space, I can only speak in generalisations, but the Victorian nobility preferred elegant, understated carving in the Gothic style. High-end carvers perfected the naturalistic portrayal of crops, garden flowers, fruit, and woodland flora, often individualised with mottos and crests. By the 1860s, breadboards became more commercial as carvers avoided time-consuming techniques such as under-carving, undulations and smooth backgrounds. Patterns became more standardised and tended towards symmetrical repeats covering half, a third or a quarter of the border. Wheat became notional, traced in briefly in the 1 shilling items.

What is the lettering like?
The Gothic Revival, which reached its peak in the nineteenth century, inspired lettering in the 'Old English' style, reflecting a nostalgia for a pre-industrial world. Towards the 1880s, square lettering is more in evidence. From the Edwardian

period onward, with the influence of the Bauhaus, breadboards followed style with clean straight lines, plain patterns and low-relief.

Is the motto rare?

There are common mottos such as 'Bread' and 'Our Daily Bread', or variations on the Christian theme of the *Credo*. Others convey homely wisdoms ('Eat of My Bread') or have a moralising tone ('Waste Not Want Not'). Breadboards were given as wedding gifts, as birthday presents, as holiday souvenirs, and even to mark professional milestones. Since breadboards were often home-made by ordinary people for personal celebrations, there's no limit to the variety of mottos that can be found.

What about mottos in other languages?

We think breadboards are an intrinsically British invention, but the fad spread around the world as the British explored, emigrated and traded. We know British carvers produced boards with 'Pain' for the French market, for example. We also know Swiss carvers made breadboards with edelweiss and English mottos, as tourist souvenirs to appeal to British visitors. The collection includes mottos in numerous languages, suggesting breadboards were an import, since these cultures had diverse bread rituals of their own including dishes and baskets, or none at all, as in the case of China.

Is there a stamp or signature on the back?

Carvers rarely signed their work as they were not considered artists. Some boards of the 1980s onwards may have the stamp of Bramhall of Sheffield, a very prolific maker, whereas others sometimes have the stamp of the retailer who wished to protect his sources. Signatures can be subtle, such as the use of a mouse in the workshop of the British furniture maker Robert Thompson (1876-1955). The carving community could identify each other by the way motifs were depicted, so each workshop would have its signature look. But even within Thompson's 'Mouseman' workshop, no two carvers would approach their mouse in exactly the same way, so it also acted as a personal signature.

Which wood is it?

Most boards are made of sycamore. Certain boards are of oak, especially those made as pilgrimage souvenirs from cathedral towns such as Winchester and Canterbury. We have also found boards of beech, fruit wood and Swiss walnut, but they are the exceptions.

Where can I find them?

Favourite hunting grounds are Kempton, Ardingly, Newark and Portobello. The Internet is also a good place to keep tabs, especially sites such as www.thesaleroom.com. Also visit the Antique Kitchen site (www.theantiquekitchen.co.uk) which posts its latest finds for sale online.

3.

Recipes

by

Marie Lester

Recipes for Breadboards

The recipes in the following pages have been selected and developed for their simplicity and flavour.

Notes for New Bakers

The magical feeling you get when you first discover how easy it is to make bread by bringing together flour, salt, water and yeast is incredible. Once tried, never forgotten. Before doing the research for this book (although I am a very keen cook) I had never made anything using yeast. Like many people, I found the idea of baking with yeast rather intimidating – as well as time-consuming – and I didn't think it would be worth the effort. I had bought good, handmade bread from a great bakery in London for many years (driving for 45 minutes to get it). But now, having made my own, there's no going back. I have stopped buying bread almost totally as homemade really IS the best.

My learning curve has been steep. I have baked, made mistakes, done a lot of reading, baked some more – and over a period of just a few months, developed a simplified approach which has helped me and I hope will help you.

Master recipe

I have established a basic master bread recipe: 500 g flour, 15 g fresh yeast, 250-350 ml of liquid and 8-10 g salt.

Varying the formula

Once you have mastered this basic bread recipe you can easily vary it.

Flour: Experiment with different flours, for example by mixing 250 g strong white bread flour with 250 g of any of the wonderful choices available: barley, rye, malt, chestnut, spelt, einkorn, emmer, chickpea, farro, enkir, buckwheat or wholemeal – just to give you an idea! You can buy special flours such as Victorian blend, which is made using a mix of 19th century bread wheat (*Triticum aestivum*), varieties which are grown organically in Buckinghamshire and Gloucestershire. Or a Viking blend of barley (*Hordeum sativum*) flour, which contains ancient six-row 'bere' barley from Orkney, and heritage lines from Scandinavia and the UK.

These ancient varieties add flavour but also tend to have lower protein levels in them than modern varieties. Get an idea of the gluten level in the flour and if it's low (like rye) use it alongside a higher gluten variety (often called 'strong' flour) to maintain the spring in your crumb! (See my recipes for Cottage Loaf and Mixed Rye Sourdough Bread.)

Liquid: You can change the liquid from solely water and enrich your bread with milk and a little fat (such as butter, lard or olive oil), which will both extend the life of your loaf and improve the texture. You can add sweetness and different flavours in the form of sugar, honey, molasses, treacle or maple syrup. (See my recipes for Cornish Saffron Bread, Maple Syrup Loaf, Greek Bread and German Brown Bread.)

Texture: You can add dried fruits, saffron and seeds for additional flavour and texture. (See my recipes for Bara Brith, Barmbrack and Cornish Saffron Bread.)

Equipment

You will need a reasonably large surface to work on, large and small mixing bowls, a set of digital scales, a thermometer, a wooden spoon, a dough cutter, a dough scraper, a lame or grignette for cutting the skin of the dough, a banneton, a thin linen cloth for covering your dough, a kitchen mixer (optional), bread tins.

Yeast

The baking of cakes and breads normally involves a raising agent. The cake recipes in the following pages require baking powder, and the breads yeast.

The array of yeasts available can be very confusing. I experimented with all of them until deciding to stick with using fresh yeast and my sourdough starter. But not everyone can get fresh yeast so an alternative needs to be found. To make it easier to understand the options, below is a table to give a quick overview.

Type	Moisture content	Keeps	To activate
Fresh yeast	70-80%	2 weeks (refrigerated)	Add lukewarm (90-100°F / 32-38°C) water before using
Active instant	3%	2 years	Activate with lukewarm (90-100°F / 32-38°C) water before using
Instant dried*	3%	2 years	Add directly to flour
Sourdough starter**	100%	If maintained, indefinitely	Keep in fridge and feed weekly if not using; feed daily for 3 days before baking with 100 g rye flour and 80-100 ml lukewarm water

You need about half the quantity of dried yeast to fresh, so a 7 g sachet of dried yeast is equivalent to 15 g fresh yeast.
**The fermentation of flour and water producing carbon dioxide (rise) and lactic acid (flavour).*

Shaping

You can vary the final shape of a loaf (or bread roll), whether it's a tin shape, a round loaf, little rolls, a plait – the choice is yours.

Scoring the dough

Scoring is the technical term for cutting the surface of the bread dough with a sharp knife or lame before baking. Scoring creates weak spots in the bread's crust and allows the bread to rise further during baking. Make quick clean cuts in the dough at a 45° angle and make them about ½ cm deep. You don't always have to score the dough. The mixed rye sourdough recipe (shown below right) has not been scored. The dough has expanded naturally and looks very appealing.

Making a sourdough starter

If you wish to make the rye bread you will need an extra ingredient known as sourdough starter, which will become the raising agent.

Day 1: Put 50 g of rye flour mixed with 50 g of water (room temperature) in a large, clean lidded jam jar (or equivalent). Allow to rest in a warm place in the kitchen with the lid just covering the jar (not screwed tight).

Days 2-5: Repeat the 'feeding' process each day (don't refrigerate at this stage).

Over the 5-day period the starter will mature. On day 6 the starter is ready for use.

Thereafter when not in use, feed the starter weekly with 100 g of rye flour and 80-100 ml lukewarm water. Place the jar with the lid on in a fridge.

The starter will bubble up and grow when it is working (the effect of carbon dioxide) and give off a strong aroma which is all the different forms of yeast being formed along with their by-products, including alcohol (ethanol) and lactic acid.

When planning to bake, take the jar out of the fridge and feed every day for 3 days prior to baking. If the jar becomes too full, empty out some of the starter and add a teaspoon of sugar to give it a boost along with its flour and water feed.

Once developed, don't leave your starter sitting at room temperature for more than three days – or in a refrigerated environment for more than one week – without refreshing it. If this happens, the acidity of the starter will be compromised and the gluten structure will not be strong enough to produce a nice light crumb. Once made, your starter will last for years if maintained correctly.

Results to look for

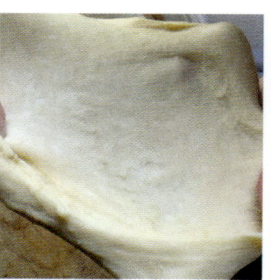
Elasticity of the dough after kneading, which you can test by stretching it out thinly

A good rise of the dough when left in a warm place

An even golden brown colour after baking

A consistent crumb

A crunchy crust

A good flavour

A loaf needs a hot, moist environment initially to create a crispy crust and the best way to do this is to create some steam.

Using an ordinary domestic oven, first preheat to the required temperature. Place a tray at the bottom of the oven and put a cup or two of water in it just before you put your loaf in the oven. This will create steam.

Place your loaf on a baking stone or baking tray, lined with baking paper. The stone or tray should be positioned immediately above the tray of water. Cover the loaf with a tall metal bowl. Alternatively place on the lid of a Dutch oven (covered with baking paper) and place the casserole bowl over it upside down.

After this, the loaf needs a dry baking environment, so remove the cover or lid. If the water in the tray at the bottom of the oven hasn't all evaporated, carefully remove it from the oven at this point.

Bake the loaf for another 20-25 minutes until golden brown. (Further note: don't spray the bread with water as this just cools the surface of the loaf.)

The loaf must be properly baked for maximum life. To check that your loaf is cooked, tap it underneath – it will sound hollow.

The way you cool and store your bread after baking is very important. Immediately after you have taken the loaf out of the oven, remove the baking paper from underneath.

Cool on a wire rack allowing air to circulate under the loaf. Once cool, wrap the loaf in a clean linen cloth. The linen will naturally absorb the moisture which continues to travel from the inside of the loaf to the outer crust. A paper bag is the next best form of wrapping – basically any wrapping which allows the bread to breathe!

Keep the loaf inside a wooden bread bin or drawer, or failing that, a bread bin that is well-aerated. If you don't have a bread bin, use a plastic bag but don't seal it.

Keep the bread in a cool environment (but not in the fridge). It should keep well for about 3 days.

But the best way to stop your bread going stale is quite simply to eat it!

Plain Scones

Difficulty level

Scones are quintessentially English and part of British culinary history. References to them date back to the early 16th century. This is not so surprising as they are one of the delights of culinary alchemy. Take some flour, baking powder, butter, sugar – add some milk – and like magic you can create a treat for tea.

In addition, everyone can discuss whether one should say 'scon' or 'scone' and whether to put the jam on first (Cornwall) or the cream on first (Devon). But be aware that if you are invited for tea at Buckingham Palace, it's jam first!

So a baking delight, an ice-breaker – and a totally customisable treat if you serve your guests with a selection of jams and creams (crème fraîche is a very tasty alternative to clotted cream).

Ingredients:

500 g plain white flour (fine, 00-type, or a soft cake and pastry flour)
25 g baking powder
Large pinch salt
100 g golden caster sugar

150 g cold butter diced
225-250 ml semi-skimmed milk

Milk to glaze

Method:

Preheat an oven to 180°C / 360°F / Gas Mark 4/5. Put the flour, baking powder and salt into a large bowl and stir to combine. Add the diced butter and rub it into the flour until the mixture has the consistency of coarse breadcrumbs.

Using a knife, stir in the sugar, then the milk, adding it a bit at a time (different flours absorb liquid differently). Use your hand to bring all the ingredients together to form a dough. You will then be able to feel how much liquid is needed. Cover with a clean cloth and leave to rest for 10-15 minutes.

On a lightly-floured surface, bring the mix together into a ball, flatten into a disc and then press out using a rolling pin to a thickness of 2-3 cm. Take a sharp 5 cm cutter, dip it into flour and cut out around 15 scones. Don't twist the cutter as this will distort the scones as they rise. Place the scones on a baking tray lined with baking parchment. If you place the scones close together, this will encourage them to rise!

Using a pastry brush, glaze the tops of the scones with milk. Don't glaze the sides as this will prevent them from rising as much.

Place in a hot oven for 10-15 minutes until the scones are risen and golden brown. Cool on a rack and dust with snow or icing sugar.

Scones are best eaten on the same day that you bake them as they don't keep. You can freeze them, but after defrosting give them a couple of minutes in a medium oven to refresh them before eating.

A United Kingdom Breadboard

Decorated with the floral insignia of England, Scotland, and Ireland.
Sycamore, circa 1870, 13 inches.

Difficulty level

The Cottage Loaf

Variants of this loaf include the small top cottage loaf, the cottage loaf, and the brick – depending on how large the 'top' of the loaf is. Anecdotally, the origin of this strange two-tiered structure is thought to be a space-saving innovation: in the days before ovens in the home, villagers took their loaves to the local bakehouse where they were placed on top of each other – making them look like a dwelling. And so the name 'cottage' loaf was born.

Mrs Beeton in her eponymously named cookery book, first published in 1861, shows a drawing of a cottage loaf on a bread-platter. The shape is similar to the French brioche and also to the pain chapeau.

COTTAGE LOAF.

Ingredients:

500 g organic strong white bread flour.
For a brown loaf use 300 g strong white bread flour and 200 g wholemeal flour.
For a more authentic loaf (as pictured) use 300 g strong white bread flour and 200 g heritage 'Victorian Blend White Flour' (available online)

8 g salt

15 g fresh yeast (or 7 g sachet of dried yeast)

40 g grated lard (or butter)

250-270 g lukewarm water (90-100°F / 32-38°C)
Note: wholemeal flour requires more water to make the dough

4 g sugar

Method:

Dissolve the fresh yeast into 50 g of the water. Add the sugar. Let it sit for 10 minutes until it starts to bubble. This shows that the yeast is active. If using dried yeast, add the yeast to the flour in the next stage.

Mix the flours and salt in a large mixing bowl. Add the lard (or butter, if you prefer). Add all the water plus the yeasty mixture to the flour and bring together using your hand shaped like a claw (or a dough whisk, if you have one), until a dough starts to form. Turn the dough out onto a lightly-floured surface and knead for 10 minutes.

Roughly shape the dough into a ball by cupping your hands around it at the bottom and turning, and then place into a lightly-greased bowl. Cover with a clean, slightly damp cloth to stop a crust forming on it and allow to rest for 1 to 1 ½ hours (or until doubled in size).

Turn the dough out onto a lightly-floured surface and gently remove the gas that has formed by flattening the dough with your fingers. Cut ⅓ of the flattened dough away.

Take the largest piece of dough: take hold of the edge furthest away and fold it back towards you onto the dough, not quite to the edge, and press gently. Turn 45° and repeat. Do this several times until the dough becomes a tight ball. Turn the dough over so that the folded-in 'ends' are on the bottom. Repeat with the smaller piece of dough.

Taking each piece of dough, create a little more surface tension by cupping your hands around the ball, turning and tucking under simultaneously. Place the larger ball of dough on a baking tray lined with baking parchment. Place the smaller round ball directly on top of the larger piece. Dust the loaf with a little flour then, using two fingers (also dusted with flour), make a vertical hole straight through both dough balls. Now cover with a light, clean cloth and leave for 45-60 minutes. Preheat the oven to 220°C / 425°F / Gas Mark 7.

Remove the cloth and using a baker's lame or grignette (a dough cutter), cut the dough at intervals around the sides, top and bottom. Put a deep tray on the bottom shelf, place 2 cups of water in it and close the oven door immediately. This creates a little steam which will help a good crust to develop. Next place the baking tray with the loaf in the oven, just above the tray with water.

Bake for 20 minutes and then turn down the heat to 190°C / 375°F / Gas Mark 6 and bake for a further 15-20 minutes. When it is golden brown, take it out and tap the base to check that it is ready. It should sound hollow. Cool on a wire rack.

Difficulty level

Bara Brith

This is a very simple but oh so tasty fruit cake from Wales called Bara Brith which literally means "mottled bread".

There are two traditional recipes for this, one which uses yeast and the other which does not. The first is more like a bread and the second more like a cake. Both are delicious sliced and served with plenty of butter.

The following recipe is the yeast-free version so it's very quick. But the day before you make it, the fruit needs be to soaked in black tea. This adds flavour and makes the cake beautifully moist.

Ingredients:

*400 g dried
mixed fruit*
300 ml warm black tea

*150 g muscovado sugar
(or brown sugar)*
1 tsp mixed spice
½ tsp cinnamon
250 g self-raising flour
1 egg, beaten

Method:

In a large bowl, soak the fruit in strained tea and leave overnight.

Next day, preheat the oven to 180°C / 360°F / Gas Mark 4/5.

Grease a large 900 g / 2 lb loaf tin, and line the bottom with baking parchment (sticking it to the sides with little dabs of butter).

Mix the remaining ingredients and add to the fruit mixture and beat well.

Pour the mixture into the tin and bake for 1 to 1½ hours, or until a cocktail stick inserted into the middle comes out clean.

Allow to cool in the tin for 10 minutes and then place on a cooling rack. Remove the baking parchment. Slice and serve with cold butter.

Wrap in foil to keep moist and place in a cake tin. This cake keeps extremely well.

A Welsh Breadboard

Decorated with the motto '*Ein Bara Beunyddiol*' ([Give us this day] our daily bread).
Oak with a curved foot, circa 1900, 12 inches.

Barmbrack Loaf

Difficulty level

Traditionally Barmbrack was made on the festival of *Samhain* which is old Irish for Summer's End. This Celtic festival merged with the Scottish festival of All Hallows' Even (known today as Halloween). Barm comes from an old English word *'beorma'* meaning bread or leavened with yeast. Brack comes from Irish *'brac'* meaning speckled.

Traditionally the ingredients would have included a few extras: a pea, a piece of cloth, a coin, a ring. If the lucky recipient found one of these in their slice it would reveal what Fate had in store for them: a pea for would mean you wouldn't marry that year, whereas a ring would let you know that you would!

There are two versions of this speckled loaf: the bread version below, made with yeast, is known as 'bracks', and the fruit cake version (where the fruit is soaked in tea similar to Bara Brith) is called 'tea bracks'. This recipe is a light and fruity loaf.

Ingredients:

150 ml milk
25 g butter
50 g golden caster sugar
1 egg, beaten

15 g of fresh yeast (or
7 g dried yeast)

300 g strong white
flour
7 g mixed spice
2 g salt

200 g mixed dried
fruit, (sultanas, raisins
and currants)
30 g mixed candied
peel

Method:

Heat the milk in a pan until lukewarm (90-100°F / 32-38°C). Add about 50 ml of the milk to the yeast in a bowl and leave to dissolve. Use a thermometer to determine the right temperature otherwise the milk might get too hot and kill the yeast.

Add the butter and sugar to the rest of the milk. Stir until melted. Whisk in the egg.

In a large bowl, mix the flour, mixed spice and salt. Add all the wet ingredients to the flour and mix together until a dough consistency is reached.

Turn the dough out onto a well-floured work surface and knead for 10 minutes.

Put the dough into a lightly-oiled 900 g / 2 lb loaf tin. Cover with a slightly damp cloth and leave in a warm place for 60 minutes, or until doubled in size.

Turn the dough out and flatten using your fingers. Scatter a handful of dried fruit and mixed peel over the dough. Fold the fruit in by rolling the dough. Flatten and repeat this process until all the fruit is incorporated.

Put the dough into a lightly-oiled 900 g / 2 lb loaf tin. Cover with a slightly damp cloth and leave for 30 minutes.

Preheat the oven to 180°C / 350°F / Gas Mark 4. Bake for 45-60 minutes. It is cooked when the loaf sounds hollow when tapped underneath.

Remove from the oven and cool on a rack and serve sliced with butter. This loaf is best eaten on the same day or can be enjoyed toasted.

An Irish Breadboard

Clover leaves, lightly engraved by a patriotic hobbyist.
Sycamore, circa 1930, 12 inches.

Cornish Saffron Loaf

Difficulty level

Saffron comes from the plant *Crocus Sativus*, which is indigenous to the near East. Saffron is associated with countries such as Iran and Spain than with Britain, but it is also grown in England. Brought over by the Romans. Saffron growing was established in Cornwall in both the Bude and Mount's Bay areas, and also in the east of England around Cambridgeshire and Essex (Saffron Waldon takes its name from it). This expensive spice was widely used in British cookery between 1600 and 1700. However, the emergence of

other cheaper spices in 1700 led to a national decline in saffron use, with the exception of Cornwall, where it continued to be used in traditional saffron-flavoured buns and in recipes such as this wonderful sunshine-yellow loaf.

Ingredients:

450 g strong white bread flour
50 g ground almonds
4 g salt
1 g of freshly grated nutmeg
2 g cinnamon
50 g golden caster sugar

300 ml milk
1 tsp saffron threads
15 g fresh yeast /
7 g dry yeast
75 g melted butter

50 g golden sultanas
50 g currants

Glaze for the loaf top
1 tbsp sugar
2 tbsp milk

Method:

Heat the milk in a pan and remove just before it boils. Pour ¾ over the saffron strands into a small bowl and leave to infuse for between 30-60 minutes (until you have a good yellow colour). Let the rest of the milk cool to lukewarm temperature (90-100°F / 32-38°C) and then mix in the yeast and leave for 10 minutes until little bubbles appear. You can add a pinch of sugar to help it along.

Mix the dry ingredients together in a bowl. Add the saffron infusion, the yeast mixture and the melted butter and mix together until a sticky dough forms.

Turn out onto a lightly-floured surface and knead until smooth. Place in a lightly-oiled bowl and cover with a damp cloth. Leave in a warm place for 1 ½ to 2 hours, until doubled in size. Turn out the dough onto a lightly-floured surface and press out the air using your fingers. Lay some of the currants and golden sultanas over the dough and fold over. Repeat the process until all the fruit is used up. Divide into two, roll each piece into a log shape and place into two lightly-oiled 500 g / 1 lb baking tins. Cover with a damp cloth and leave for another 1 ½ hours or until the dough has risen to the top of the tins.

Preheat the oven to 220°C / 425°F / Gas Mark 7. Place the loaves near the bottom of the oven and bake for 10 minutes. Reduce the temperature to 180°C / 360°F / Gas Mark 4/5 and bake for another 10 minutes until golden. Cover the top with foil if the top of the loaf is getting too brown – this loaf bakes very quickly!

Prepare the glaze by dissolving the sugar in the milk in a pan on a low heat. Remove the loaves from the oven and brush the tops with the glaze using a pastry brush. Leave to cool for 5 minutes in the tins then turn out onto a cooling rack. Slice and serve with cold butter. Cornish Saffron bread is very good toasted 2-3 days after baking.

A Celtic Breadboard

Decorated with the iconic Celtic knot finished off with dragon heads, acorns and oak leaves.
Sycamore, circa 1880, 12 inches.

Difficulty level

Mixed Rye Sourdough Bread

Rye bread has always been associated with the colder Nordic countries, the high valleys of the Alps and of course Germany. It is very popular today for its health properties. It is high in lysine, a good source of zinc, copper, manganese and selenium, and a very good source of dietary fibre.

Rye flour is low gluten so this bread doesn't rise in the same way as a loaf made with a strong wheat flour. This recipe therefore uses a mixture of flours which creates a very nice flavour and texture and is delicious with salad, cold sliced beef and fish, especially Scottish smoked salmon.

Ingredients:

250 g light rye flour
250 g strong white bread flour

5 g fresh baker's yeast
10 g salt

200 g sourdough starter (see new baker's notes)

350 ml lukewarm (90-100°F / 32-38°C) water

Method:

Mix all the ingredients in an electric mixer (KitchenAid or similar) for 10-15 minutes using the dough hook. Put what will be a very sticky dough in a lightly-oiled bowl. Leave to rest for 2-3 hours or until doubled in size. Fold the dough every 30 minutes to help create structure in the gluten as it forms. You can also cover and refrigerate overnight for a slower rise (8 hours).

Turn out the dough onto a lightly-floured surface. Fold to push out the air that has formed. Shape the dough into a ball, folding the outer corners into the middle. This helps to create surface tension.

Flour and put into a well-floured banneton (seam facing upwards) and leave to proof for an hour (or until the dough has risen to the top of the banneton).

Preheat the oven to 220°C / 425°F / Gas Mark 7. Put a deep baking tray into the bottom of the oven. Turn the dough out from the banneton directly onto a baking tray lined with baking paper. Dust the top of the dough lightly with flour. You can score with a lame to create a pattern or leave (as illustrated) for a more natural effect. Cover with the bowl of an upturned Dutch oven casserole.

Put 1-2 cups of cold water into the baking tray at the bottom of the oven. Put the shaped dough straight into the oven on the baking tray, just above the tray of water. Close the oven immediately to contain the steam.

Bake for 20 minutes at 220°C / 425°F / Gas Mark 7 then remove the casserole bowl and bake for a further 15-20 minutes at 180°C / 350°F / Gas Mark 4, until the loaf sounds hollow when tapped underneath. Cool on a wire rack, slice and enjoy.

An Anglo-Scottish Bread-Platter

Unique for its floral emblems proud of the rim, this platter may have been a commemoration of the Union of 1706, or a wedding present for a couple of dual heritage. The handles and basket weave depression are reminiscent of Scottish quaitches, while the harvest border represents English breadboard traditions. Sycamore, circa 1880, 16 inches.

Greek Bread

Difficulty level

This handsome loaf is based on recipes for *tsoureki*. The bread is enriched with eggs and butter which not only add flavour but also give the bread a lovely soft texture (not unlike brioche).

Ingredients:

For the sponge:
15 g fresh yeast
(or 7 g dried yeast)
50 g strong white bread flour
10 g golden caster sugar
50 ml semi-skimmed milk

2 large eggs
250 ml semi-skimmed milk
40 g golden caster sugar
60 g unsalted butter, melted

450-500 g strong white bread flour
4 g salt

1 egg, beaten, for glazing

Sesame seeds for sprinkling (optional)

Method:

Heat the milk in a pan until lukewarm (90-100°F / 32-38°C). Mix the fresh yeast with a little of the warm milk, sugar and flour in a bowl. Let stand in a warm place for 10 minutes or so, until the mixture is bubbly and foaming.

Mix the eggs, the rest of the sugar and milk, and stir well. Add this to the yeast mixture along with the melted butter.

Put 450 g of the flour into another bowl with the salt. Make a well in the middle and pour in the wet mixture. Bring the sticky mixture together adding small amounts of additional flour as necessary until you have a dough. Knead until smooth on a floured surface for 8-10 minutes. Place the dough in a lightly-oiled bowl, cover with a clean damp tea towel and leave in a warm place to rise for about 1 ½ hours, or until doubled in size.

Gently punch the dough back and tip out on to a lightly-floured surface.

Grease a 30 cm / 12 inch round tin and line it with baking parchment (otherwise the bread will stick to the tin). Cut off a quarter of the dough and divide into four smaller portions. Roll each portion between the palms of your hands into a length. Twist two lengths of dough together. Repeat.

Line the sides of the tin with the twisted lengths of dough. Shape the remaining dough into a ball and place it in the centre of the tin, leaving a gap between the twisted lengths and the central ball to allow for expansion. Cover with a tea towel and leave in a warm place for 30 minutes.

Preheat the oven to 200°C / 400°F / Gas Mark 6. Brush the dough with whisked egg and sprinkle with sesame seeds. Bake for about 30-40 minutes. Cover with foil during the last 15 minutes of baking to prevent burning. If the bread sounds hollow when tapped underneath, it is cooked. Allow to cool for 5 minutes before removing from the tin. Ease out gently and leave to cool completely on a wire rack.

A Greek Breadboard

Carved with the motto: τὸν ἄρτον ἡμῶν τὸν ἐπιούσιον δὸς ἡμῖν σήμερον
(Give us this day our daily bread).
Sycamore, circa 1900, 14 inches (Marie Lester Collection).

Difficulty level

Maple Syrup White Tin Loaf

A freshly baked loaf of bread is a treat in any household. This recipe is for a white loaf of bread – much maligned in recent years. But when you make it yourself, you choose exactly what goes into it. No preservatives; no environmentally damaging palm oil; no emulsifiers; no reducing agent; no soya flour, no chlorine dioxide (bleach!) and no hydrogenated or fractionated fats. Just good wholesome ingredients.

What this recipe does include is maple syrup which adds an extra dimension. As well as adding a little sweetness, maple syrup adds its own unique and subtle flavour. And if your loaf is not all eaten in one sitting, this bread is wonderful toasted with pâté or cheese – or best of all – use it to make a toasted bacon 'buttie' (English slang for sandwich).

Ingredients:

250 ml milk
60 g unsalted butter
50 ml maple syrup

60 ml lukewarm water
15 g fresh yeast

1 egg whisked

500 g Canadian strong white bread flour

1 tsp salt

Method:

Heat the milk, butter and maple syrup gently in a saucepan until melted. Allow to cool until it is lukewarm (90-100°F / 32-38°C).

Mix the yeast with the water and allow to stand while the milk mixture is cooling.

In a large bowl, mix the milk and maple syrup mixture with the yeasty liquid. Stir in the egg. Stir in flour and salt, and mix until a dough starts to form.

Turn the dough out onto a lightly-floured surface, and knead for 8-10 minutes until it is smooth and elastic. Place the dough in a lightly-oiled bowl and cover with a damp cloth. Leave to rise in a warm place for 1-2 hours, or until the dough has doubled in size.

Gently knock back the dough and turn out onto a lightly-floured surface. Flatten using your finger tips and shape into a rectangle. Then roll the rectangle up and tuck the ends under. Place in a large, lightly-oiled, rectangular bread tin, positioning the seam at the bottom. Lightly flour the top of the dough and make a deep cut in the surface from end to end using a lame or very sharp knife.

Cover with a damp cloth and leave to rise for 30-60 minutes until well-risen. Heat the oven to 190°C / 375°F / Gas Mark 5. Bake for 35–45 minutes, until the loaf looks golden brown and sounds hollow when tapped underneath. Cool on a wire rack for at least 30 minutes, then slice it on your breadboard of choice.

A Canadian Breadboard

Intended as a wall plaque, this breadboard may have been embellished for the tourist market. Morning Glory, a common flower of North America, decorates the border, while the cutting surface depicts a Canadian lakeside scene. Hardwood and oil, unsigned, circa 1900, 13 inches.

Difficulty level

Corn Meal Rolls

Soft little corn meal rolls are practical for appetites great and small. Fill them with ham and pickle, cheese and coleslaw or mixed salad and adaptable to all sorts of family occasions such as barbecues, picnics and birthdays.

Ingredients:

250 ml milk
60 g unsalted butter

60 ml lukewarm water
15 g fresh yeast

1 egg whisked

250 g strong white bread flour
250 g maize flour
8 g salt

Coarse maize flour for flouring (optional)

Method:

Heat the milk and butter gently in a saucepan until melted. Allow to cool until lukewarm (90-100°F / 32-38°C). Mix the yeast with the water and allow to stand while the milk mixture is cooling.

Mix the flours and salt together in a large bowl. Add the milk mixture, the whisked egg and the yeasty liquid. Shaping your hand like a claw, turn the mixture in your hand until a dough consistency is reached.

Turn the dough out onto a lightly-floured surface, and knead for 10 minutes. It will be sticky but try to avoid adding extra flour. Work until the dough is smooth and elastic. Place the dough in a lightly-oiled bowl and cover with a damp cloth. Leave to rise in a warm place for 1–2 hours, or until the dough has doubled in size.

Gently punch the dough down in the bowl then turn out and knead for a few minutes. Cut the dough in half and each piece in half again. Repeat until you have roll-size pieces. Weigh each piece to ensure that the rolls are equal in size. Aim for 60 g apiece – this will help them to cook evenly. You should get at least 12 balls of dough. Shape each piece of dough into a ball shape by drawing an outer edge of the dough into the centre, turning by 45 degrees and then repeating. All the ends should end up in the centre. Turn over the roll so that the ends are on the bottom and place on a baking tray, lined with baking paper. Cover with a damp cloth and leave to rise for another 30 minutes until well-risen.

Heat the oven to 190°C / 375°F / Gas 5. Dust the rolls with some coarse maize flour. Place in the hot oven and bake for 15-20 minutes, until the rolls look golden brown and sound hollow when tapped underneath.

Cool on a wire rack for at least 30 minutes and then arrange the rolls on your breadboard of choice.

An American Board

This board features the Seven Dwarfs, skilfully portrayed in the style of the Disney film, *Snow White*. The board also has a decorative motif around the edge of running rabbits.
Sycamore, 20th century, circa second quarter, 11 inches (Marie Lester Collection).

Difficulty level

Spicy Banana Bread

Almost all African countries grow bananas and spices, so it is not surprising that many also have a recipe for a bread which combines both. The East coast of Africa has had a strong spice trade since ancient times due to the sea-going trade developed by the peoples living around the Indian Ocean. Spices from Asia arrived in Zanzibar (now Tanzania) long before the European spice merchants started trading in spices. Zanzibar's hot climate and rainfall made it ideal as a location for spice farming, which rapidly became Zanzibar's main source of income.

The use of spices in English cooking dates back to at least the 14th century. A cookery book called *The Forme of Cury* (meaning 'method of cooking') mentions both mace and cloves. The English developed their taste for spices further as a result of Indian cuisine.

Spices have long since fascinated people for their health-giving properties. There seems to be a spice cure for just about anything. This moist loaf should act as a cure-all as it contains a wide variety!

Ingredients:

175 g unsalted butter
175 g golden caster sugar
3 large eggs, beaten

150 g plain flour
25 g ground almonds
50 g wholemeal or spelt flour
1 tsp salt
2 tsp baking powder

1 tsp cinnamon
1 tsp nutmeg
1 tsp ginger
½ tsp cloves

100 ml milk

2 large ripe bananas

Method:

Take the butter out of the fridge and allow to soften.

Preheat oven to 180°C / 350°F / Gas Mark 4.

Using a whisk or mixer, beat the butter and sugar together until light and fluffy. Add the eggs, flour and almonds, whisking all the time. Add the baking powder, spices, salt and milk, and whisk until smooth.

Mash the bananas and stir in.

Pour the mixture into a 900 g / 2 lb loaf tin with baking parchment. Bake for 45-60 minutes until golden brown.

To test when the spiced banana bread is cooked, insert a cocktail stick into the cake. When it comes out clean it is ready.

Leave in the tin for 15 minutes, then lift out and cool completely on a rack.

An East African Board

An octagonal board, decorated with geometric tribal patterns.
Sapele wood, 13 inches.

Difficulty level

Brown Bread (Braunbrot)

This recipe for 'brown' bread is inspired by the German Braunbrot. The addition of molasses, rapeseed oil and cocoa add new flavours which are hard to pinpoint but which create a depth of flavour. The resultant bread looks English on the outside but tastes continental on the inside. This is a great companion to cheese and strong meats like salami and also works well toasted with scrambled egg and smoked salmon for breakfast.

Ingredients:

15 g fresh baker's yeast
80 ml lukewarm water

150 g brown wholemeal wheat flour
350 g strong white bread flour
7 g / 1 tbsp cocoa
10 g salt

50 g molasses
50 g rapeseed oil
5-10 g honey
150 ml lukewarm water

Method:

Dissolve the yeast into 80 ml of lukewarm water.

Sieve the wholemeal flour into a mixing bowl. Add the white flour. Add back some of the sieved bran and reserve the rest. Mix the molasses, rapeseed oil, a dash of honey and 150 ml lukewarm water in a jug.

Mix the flours together then add the yeasty liquid and the molasses mixture to the bowl. Mix together shaping your hand like a claw, until a sticky dough forms.

Turn the dough out onto a lightly-floured surface and knead until the dough becomes smooth and elastic (about 8-10 minutes). Shape the dough into a ball and place in a lightly-oiled bowl. Cover the bowl with a clean damp cloth and leave until doubled in size (1 to 1 ½ hours).

Gently punch the air out of the dough and turn out on to a lightly-floured surface. Flatten the dough out with your finger tips, creating a rectangle and roll. Tuck the ends under. Place into a 900 g / 2 lb loaf tin with the seam at the bottom. Leave to rise for 45-60 minutes.

Sprinkle with some of the reserved bran.

Put in to a preheated oven 200°C / 400°F / Gas Mark 6/7. Bake for 20 minutes then remove from the tin and put back into the oven on its side for 5 minutes. Turn on to the other side and repeat for a further 5 minutes.

Leave to cool on a rack.

A German Breadboard

Decorated with the motto '*Gib Uns Heute Unser Täglich Brot*' (Give us this day our daily bread).
Fruitwood, circa 1900 (Marie Lester Collection).

Difficulty level

Swiss Fondue Bread

Fondue bread is a visual delight. Created to be eaten with one of Switzerland's national dishes. Surprisingly, though, it is not known to all Swiss people. The little chunks of bread accompany the cheese fondue, made of equal quantities of gruyère, appenzeller and emmentaler cheeses, a little cornflower, dry white wine, a pinch of freshly-grated nutmeg and salt. Complement the rich cheese sauce with fresh ice berg lettuce, tomatoes and cucumber, some sharp pickles, such as gherkins and

pickled onions, and some potatoes roasted in garlic and rosemary – and you have a feast. The 'do-it-yourself' aspect is fun and promotes interaction. All-in-all an easy and highly sociable supper.

Ingredients:

250 g white flour
8 g salt

250 ml light olive oil

10 g fresh yeast
250 ml water
Pinch of sugar

Method:

Mix the flour and salt together in a bowl. In a separate bowl, dissolve the fresh yeast in the water along with a large pinch of sugar.

Add the olive oil and the yeasty water to the flour and mix until you have a dough. Knead the dough for 8-10 minutes until smooth.

Place the dough in a lightly-oiled bowl, cover with a damp cloth and leave in a warm place to rise for 1 ½ to 2 hours, until it doubles in size. Turn out onto a lightly-floured surface.

Flatten with your fingers to remove the air. Gently roll out to 1 cm thickness. Place on a baking tray which has been lined with baking parchment.

Using a large knife or pizza cutter, cut the dough into squares, cutting almost all the way through the dough.

Cover the dough with a damp cloth and let it rest for another 30 minutes until it has risen again. Brush the surface with water and dust with flour.

Preheat the oven to 180°C / 350°F / Gas Mark 4, and bake for 30 minutes on the bottom shelf of the oven. It is cooked when the loaf sounds hollow when tapped underneath. Remove from the oven and cool on a rack.

Tear or cut the appealing little chunks of bread and enjoy with your Swiss cheese fondue.

A Swiss Breadboard

Carved with an edelweiss border and the motto 'Give us this day our daily bread'.
Fruitwood, circa 1880, 13 inches (Marie Lester Collection).

4.

Mottos & Motifs

Status Symbols

The early boards were very ornate, and were intended as display items 'front of house' to impress guests, with patrons spending between 12 shillings – 4 guineas per board. This section shows how past owners used their boards to boost their status. Although Mrs Beeton does not mention breadboards in the first edition of *Beeton's Book of Household Management* of 1861, George Wing was already popularising them with his cheaper versions. Later editions of Beeton's book devoted half a page to a very finely carved board and its accompanying knife, and also included a breadboard in an illustration accompanying a country house breakfast spread 'Suitable for twelve persons'. It proposed a cottage loaf as a back-up, in case guests ate their way through all the delights on the table! But Mrs Beeton may have been presenting an idyll. On a visit to Polesden Lacey, the Edwardian house and estate run by the National Trust, I asked about the breakfast room, wondering if they had a breadboard displayed as Mrs Beeton had instructed. The answer was: the guests were so hungover from the evening's excitements, that breakfast was rarely served!

Mrs Beeton's formal breakfast for twelve, from a later edition of
Mrs Beeton's Book of Household Management.

But bread-platters also had an informal role at 'family tea'. For these 'eminently feminine meals where children are not excluded by reason of age', the parents would eat together with their offspring, without the servants in attendance, and Mama would take charge of pouring tea and cutting bread as required. 'Shall I be Mum?' is a quirky phrase still used by men and women alike at informal gatherings to get the food and drink flowing, including slicing bread.

3201. *Family teas* most often consist of cake, preserve, sardines, potted meats, buttered toast, tea cakes and fruit, in addition to the tea, coffee, and bread and butter. Watercress and radishes are nice accompaniments in summer, and these eminently feminine meals may be very pleasant ones, from which the young folks are never excluded by reason of age, as they would be at a late dinner.

The hours for family teas may vary in many households, but are generally governed by the time of the dinner that has preceded them, and the kind of supper partaken of afterwards. Where this is of a very light character, such as a glass of wine and a slice of cake, or the more homely glass of beer and bread and cheese, a 6 to 7 o'clock tea would not be late, and a few little savouries or eggs would be needed in addition to the bread and butter and cake so generally found; but where a substantial supper is to follow the tea the latter would be of a very light description and might be served as early as 5 to 6 o'clock

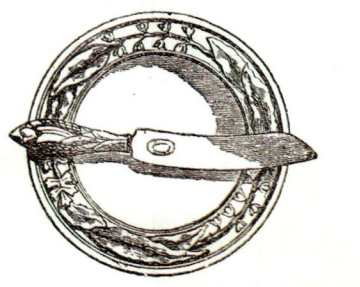

'Family tea', from *Mrs Beeton's Book of Household Management,* 1886 edition.

Bread-platter motifs chimed in with the latest interior design fads, echoing furniture and fixtures. The laurel design on this composite mould (below) by George Jackson – used to embellish chimney pieces, frames, mirrors and doors – bears a striking resemblance to the motifs running around certain bread-platters.

Composite moulding, George Jackson, boxwood, 15 x 3 ½ inches, 1780-90s, beside the Jubilee board.

A handful of boards can be traced back to their owners who bought one of these latest must-haves, and Rosslyn had great fun piecing together their stories.

Sarah Sophia Child (1785-1867)

Sarah Sophia, the Countess of Jersey, ordered our oldest board from William Gibbs Rogers to celebrate her judicious marriage into the aristocracy (see WGR section for the photo), with four capital 'J's carved as entwined ivy for her Jersey in-laws. The two opposing Earl's coronets, distinguishable by five rays and topped with balls, refer to her and her husband's titles of Earl and Countess. The mirror-image effect of the 'J's suggests her marriage partnership. The word 'Middleton', carved in elegant Gothic style, was her family seat at Middleton Park, in Middleton Stoney, Oxfordshire, now rebuilt.

Sarah Sophia was the oldest grand-daughter of Robert Child, a banking magnate at the head of Child & Co. On his death in 1782, Child disinherited his daughter (Sarah Sophia's mother), because she had eloped to Gretna Green with John Fane, 10th Earl of Westmoreland, whom he detested. Instead – and somewhat unusually for the time – Child's vast fortune was settled on Sarah Sophia, making her one of the richest women in England.

Sarah-Sophia Child-Villiers, by Frederick Christian Lewis, 1839 National Portrait Gallery, London.

Middleton Park, by J.P. Neale. © British Library Board. All Rights Reserved/Bridgeman Images.

The Parker Dynasty of Saltram House, Devon

Probably commissioned by or presented to John Parker, first Earl of Morley, this board is a proud heraldic display of pedigree, carved with the family motto *FIDELI CERTA MERCES* (There is a sure reward to the faithful). The Parker crest of a hand holding a stag's antler is also included: 'A Cubit Arm erect couped below the elbow, the sleeve Azure, cuffed and slashed Argent, the hand grasping a Stag's Attire Gules'.

Left: John Parker, 1st Earl of Morley (1772-1840) by Frederick Say (1805-1860), oil on canvas. National Trust Image. Right: The Morley board, Saltram, Devon. National Trust/Sophia Farley & Denis Madge.

Funnily enough, the first Earl was briefly married to Sarah Sophia Child's sister, Augusta Fane. His daughter, by his second marriage, married a Villiers, possibly through the matchmaking efforts of Augusta and Sarah Sophia! He was a peer of the realm and served as Lord in Waiting to Queen Victoria. Rosslyn's notes on her sketch of the board's motto (below) read: 'Splendid seriphs. I'm not exaggerating the kicks on the seriphs of the C. Two disfiguring water stains.'

Alfred Lord Tennyson, Poet Laureate, (1809-1892)
This platter is reinforcing his stature as a celebrity but is also a memento of his lost childhood. Rosslyn took great pains to visit Lincolnshire and document this stunning work of art. Alfred Lord Tennyson, son of a Rector, grew up at Somersby Rectory, Lincolnshire, where he was very happy, but was forced to leave in 1837, after the death of his father. On the occasion of his marriage thirteen years later to Emily Sellwood, he received this majestic bread-platter from Mrs Burton of Somersby Grange, wife of the lord of the Manor.

The wedding board (below) was carved by Thomas Wilkinson Wallis of Louth (1821-1903). Often referred to as the 'Grinling Gibbons of the North', Wallis was described as one of the greatest wood carvers of his age, alongside the eminent carver William Gibbs Rogers (1792-1895). We are glad to have located a sample from both workshops.

In his diary for 1850, Wallis noted that he interrupted his 'Trophy of Spring' carving, destined for the Great Exhibition of 1851. It took him but a few days to carve this masterful wedding platter for the poet Lord Alfred Tennyson: 'It was carved out of a section of a sycamore tree, grown at Somersby, the poet's native place; and was carved the end way of the grain – a difficult and laborious work. The design was of wheat, with a ribbon entwined; on which, in raised letters, the following inscription was carved: "Sycamore from the lawn of Somersby Rectory." In the centre of the plain part was carved a wreath of laurel, and the poet's initials.' He was paid three and a half guineas. The laurel wreath was prophetic in that Tennyson was appointed Poet Laureate three months later.

Tennyson's wedding platter by Thomas W. Wallis, sycamore, 1850, 18 inches. Lincolnshire Country Council: Tennyson Research Centre.

George Stone Thorpe, Sculptor in Wood (active 1877-78)

George Thorpe was a budding sculptor in the 1870s – he exhibited a *Head of Christ* at the Walker Art Gallery's autumn exhibition in Liverpool in 1878 – so this board was probably used as a practice piece to hone his skills in preparation for a glittering career. Rosslyn says of him: 'I have encountered a magnificent wood carver c1880s. It is a very fine board splendidly carved, showing wheat, oats and barley.' A fun, exuberant board, it includes an unusual 'guilloche' pattern of ovals and pips. Although very worn, it is competent, but the oats are too rugged to be successful.

The reverse of the board is also unique in the collection, being incised not only with the maker's name but his title 'Sc' for Sculptor, giving the impression of self-aggrandisement. The date and even some dubious heraldry add to the feeling

Harvest board by George Thorpe, signed, dated 1875, wormed, 12 ½ inches.

it was carved for his personal use. 'Super Antiquas Vias', a metaphor for 'In the tracks of my ancestors' derives from Jeremiah, Chapter 6 verse 16. His father was a draper and may not have been able to finance his sculpting career after all, for he does not resurface.

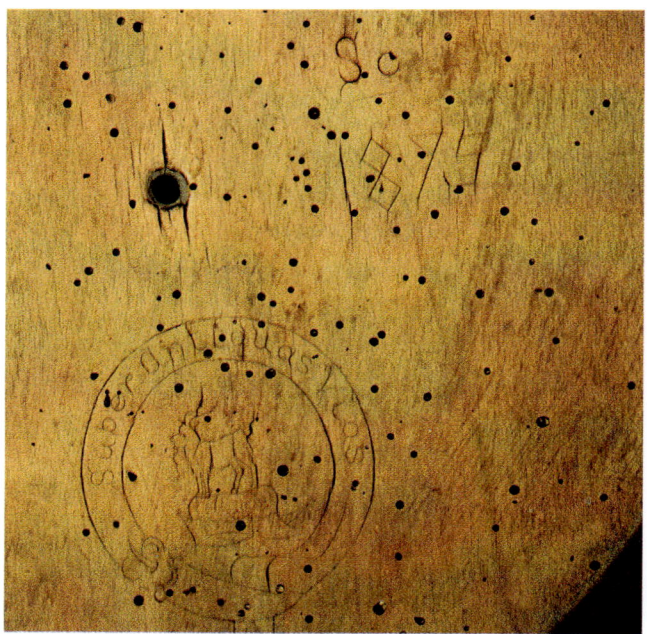

Thorpe's Harvest board (reverse), showing wormholing and graffiti.

Reverend Richard Woodfin (1820-1878)

Rev'd Richard Woodfin was rewarded for being an excellent pastor by his appreciative flock. He appears in various Wesleyan Methodist records, studying at a Wesleyan Theological Institution in Manchester in 1844. He ministered in Suffolk in 1852-3 and Walsall, Birmingham in 1854. Coincidentally, on the reverse are a number of pencilled annotations, mostly illegible, except for '1854' and possibly 'Walsall', where Methodism was flourishing.

The personalised quotation reads; 'I have planted Apollos watered but God gave the increase 1 Car. 9c. 6v.' [sic] Our local vicar, Rev'd Whittaker explained the significance of the quotation. It is an excerpt from Paul's letter to the Corinthians where he uses the metaphor of 'planting' to refer to his starting their new Church. But there is another layer of meaning. Paul was jealous of Apollos for being so successful, so he follows up his compliment to Apollos for 'watering' with a barbed comment that all his effort was immaterial as 'God gave the increase'. Rev'd Whittaker imagined that the congregation had no idea that Paul was in fact intending to belittle Apollos.

The Woodfin Board, pearwood, circa 1854, 10 inches.

The 1st Bishop of Beverley (1837-1925)

The silver plaque is a tribute to the admirable deeds of one 'RJB'. The initials refer to Robert Jarrett Crosthwaithe, the usage being to replace one's surname with the name of one's Bishopric. It reads: 'Presented to The Lord Bishop of Beverley, Selby, April 10th 1891'. The Borthwick Institute has confirmed from Crosthwaite's 'Day Book' that he was doing a work of charity that day: opening a Mission Hall. The son of a vicar, Crosthwaite rose to become the personal secretary to the Archbishop of York, and was later a 'suffragan bishop' in the diocese of York for thirty-four years (1889-1923). He also distinguished himself during his long tenure by writing 'The Gospels of the New Testament, Their Genuineness and Authenticity'.

A very heavy, impressive board, it is rather let down by a large knot. Possibly an ancient bit of beam from a local church, the wood carver must have been given it to upcycle.

Robert Jarrett Crosthwaite
National Portrait Gallery, London.

The oak motifs are perfectly symmetrical and lush in the high Victorian style. The coats of arms are of York Minster and Selby.

'RJB' bread-platter/plaque, oak, 12 ¾ inches.

The Baker Family, of Battle, Sussex

The Bakers are reminding viewers of their past victories with this shouty 'No Surrender' board, confirmed by the College of Arms. They are also drawing attention to their extensive pedigree going back ten generations from 1632. There is an interesting account entered with the pedigree stating that when Mr Baker petitioned for arms, some of his neighbours attested that he was 'noe gentleman', and the case had to go before the Lord Chamberlain, before his petition was upheld. The shield is silver and the keys and tower are black. The crest shows an arm in chain mail issuing from a black tower, the hand grasping a flintstone. The breadboard was possibly a light-hearted gesture referring to the name Baker.

A. Whitehead

While on a visit to Sheffield, Rosslyn encountered a curator at the Sheffield Galleries and Museums Trust. David Sier's father-in-law had a bread knife carved with his father's name on, which would have made a jolly talking point among guests and also a way of displaying wealth. He took the trouble of getting the story. 'It was carved by a man who came around selling them on the doorstep in Cleethorpes in 1916. The names were carved on the spot. You will notice that there is a monogram 'ER' on the blade (Edward VII: 1901-10), so they must have been old stock.'

'No Surrender', oak in three pieces, 13 inches.

A. Whitehead's bread knife, 1916, steel and sycamore.
Contributed by David Sier, Curator, Sheffield City Museum in 1998.

Belief Systems

The boards in this section are all grouped according to their mottos, which set the tone for the meal and the inner family. As boards were always present on the kitchen or dining table, they also broadcast values to guests. The selection here seems to fall into three main categories: belief in a strong, caring family; belief in God; and finally loyalty to King and Country.

A Strong, Caring Family

Family values such as hospitality and generosity, especially when celebrating marriages, house-warmings and local events, feature alongside warnings to practice thrift and self-sufficiency.

1. Generous and Fun-Loving Mottos
Encouraging your family and friends to eat is as old as the Bible, as can be seen in Proverbs 9:5: 'Come, eat my bread and drink of the wine I have mixed.' Even Ecclesiastes 8:15 concedes that given the sorry state of the human condition, 'There is nothing better for a person under the sun than to eat and to drink and to be glad.' Amen to that.

'Bread' with four wheat, sycamore, 12 inches.

Saying 'Bread'. An intriguing question that arose out of this collection was why so many breadboards and knives have the word 'Bread' on them? Carving boards and knives generally don't have 'Meat' on (although the collection does have an exception). Customers at Rosslyn's stall often asked for 'one with "Bread" on'. It feels like an echo: to give homage to the humble loaf which was unavailable to most of the population during the Corn Law period (1815-46), and a commemoration of those who starved needlessly. More radically, it could be a political statement of engrained defiance at injustice; and a warning that leaders must always deliver our human right to cheap bread, without which revolutions will again be born and rulers torn down. We might have been driven to revolution too, if Richard Cobden and his League had not reasoned the government into repealing the Corn Laws.

'Bread' with Four Wheat. A professional board, similar to those by George Wing (see 'Artists in Wood'), but made by a competitor, as the decorative elements are arranged differently. Rosslyn was a dealer while collecting, and probably had to sell most of her boards with 'BREAD' on them. This is an especially attractive example.

Homemade 'Bread'. At the other end of the spectrum, this is a good example of a homemade board showing basic carving skills, inspired by a Wing board. The lines are mostly straight and short and the lettering suggests use of one straight chisel for the entire job. The carving is shallow and flat, with patterns kept minimal. Amateur breadboards are under-represented in the collection, as Rosslyn prioritised skill. This one survived the culls because of the unusual chipping running around the cutting area, to suggest a twist.

Homemade 'Bread', beech, circa 1920, 12 inches.

Three bread knife handles, with homely mottos, ivory, sycamore and steel.

Hand in Hand. Bread knives often went hand in hand with boards, the mottos on the handle echoing those on the board.

1. 'BREAD' knife handle, the word facing in an unusual direction. A majestic lump of ivory, too cumbersome for a bread knife, except it has 'Bread' carved in, over the wheat. It is sheer virtuoso, with a bell flower on the end, and a more classical armorial on the other side. There is no sign it has ever been mounted to a blade, but it still has the original ferrule.

2. 'Bread'. An exquisite ivory handle with very expressive wheat, the slimmest chinks are visible between each grain. With a lovely texture and beautiful Gothic lettering it is joined to a frivolous steel blade suggesting it is early. James Moore 1822-1905 in Oxford Street, circa 1850.

3. 'WELCOME'. On a ribbon, with flowers poking out, Edward VII, 1901-11.

Toy Tea Sets. Where families could afford miniature tea sets, small breadboards appeared with knives to accompany the porcelain pieces. Makers used their stock of butter knives, but carved bread in the handle. They were made in doll-size also.

Pastry Sets. Miniature pastry sets also became available, so youngsters could learn the whole process, from baking to presenting. In this way our cultural heritage was being downloaded to the next generation. They are not very elaborate, as they were for the nursery.

Miniature doll's house board and knife, circa 1940, 1 ¼ inches. Private collection.

Miniature pastry set and board, 1900s, 6 x 8 inches.

Board Games. In *Mrs Beeton's Book of Household Management* there is a charming engraving called 'Twirl the Trencher' (below). According to the official rules: players sit in a round and agree a topic such as clothing. Then each player is assigned a clothing name and the first player spins the breadboard or trencher (from the French for 'slice'), shouting out one of the clothing names. The player with that name has to jump up and catch the spinning trencher before it falls and it is then their turn to call out. If they get to the trencher too late, they have to do a forfeit. It was played by adults and children alike.

'Twirl the Trencher', from *Mrs Beeton's Book of Household Management*.

Eat and be Merry. With parquetry in the Tonbridge ware style, paired with the lettering and winter twigs, this is a complete one off. The border is engraved and filled with black wax and the reverse is incised with 'Lizzie', so it is likely to have been a home-made love token. The Tonbridge-like inlay is very high quality, and would have been bought off the peg and inlaid as-is into the board by turning the background away. It was a presentation piece with almost no wear.

'Eat and Be Merry', birch, circa 1890, 11 ½ inches.

'Help Yourself'. A professionally made board, but possibly not by a bread-platter specialist. The maker may have been a carpenter, joiner, turner or cabinet-maker with access to a lathe, who made boards as a sideline, as the lettering is eccentric but charming. We cannot rule out enthusiastic woodworking members of the gentry who also had lathes made especially for their requirements. It has been much scrubbed and worn. It is the only board with this motto, although we would think it an obvious thing to write on a sharing platter.

'Dritke and Eat'. Perplexing. The beautifully calligraphied, incised lettering and wheat design make this unusual. The motto is a mystery: was it a spelling mistake for 'Drink' or an attempt at archaic spelling for an 'Olde Worlde' look, since the Victorians were nostalgic for Medievalism. Rosslyn checked with Dutch nationals, to no avail. The age of it suggests it might have been experimental, as the carver attempted to make a cheaper board, possibly round the 1860s-70s

'Help Yourself', sycamore, circa 1880, 'Dritke and Eat', sycamore, circa 1870,
12 inches. 12 inches.

when boards were in great demand across the country. Incising is much quicker than raised lettering. It was used by Bramhall, Sheffield, in the 1990s onwards, soon before it stopped production of breadboards altogether. (See 'Artists in Wood'.) The reverse has three holes where bun feet would have been.

'Eat of my Bread'. Clever. The generous moulding around the edge and many turned lines give a decorative effect without great effort, and reduce the width to carve to only an inch, which would seem meagre without the turning. It is a great combination of effect and economy. The wheat is still very pleasing with sensuous curves on the grains, and subtle hatching for an effect of shading.

'Eat of my Bread', sycamore, 13 inches.

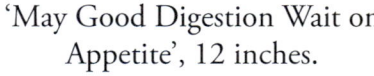

'May Good Digestion Wait on
Appetite', 12 inches.

'Cut and Come Again', sycamore
12 ½ inches.

'May Good Digestion wait on Appetite'. This phrase is a quote from Macbeth's banquet in Act III Sc iv where he is feeling too anxious to eat, waiting for news of the murders he has ordered. A strange phrase to pick one might think! These dishes weren't designed for cutting bread on, but more for serving ready-cut bread or rolls. The ceramics manufacturers were moving away from wheat to flowers. The outer ridge was good for passing the dish along, picking up and catching crumbs. The border has an inner weaving effect, representing a basket, and Gothic gilt lettering round the outside. The reverse has a splayed round foot.

'Cut and Come Again'. With ivy for friendship and unity, the lettering is eccentric for being all in capitals which gives the effect of shouting. Also note the exaggerated split serifs.

2. Parsimonious mottos and self-sufficiency
'Waste Not Want Not'(1). The border is decorated with a professional treatment of recognisable foxglove flowers. Foxgloves would have grown in hedges and were used for their digitoxin as a medicine for heart conditions, but can be a poison if doses are exceeded. The edge on this board resembles a string of sausages, which is very unusual as the sausage is normally interspersed with pips (beads). The lettering is mostly straight cuts giving a less sophisticated impression, especially the 's'.

'Waste Not Want Not' (1), sycamore, circa 1880, 11 ½ inches.

'Waste Not Want Not' (2), sycamore, 11 ½ inches.

'Waste Not Want Not' (2). Although the message calls for a Spartan lifestyle, the lettering is flamboyant, showing an artist having fun with bold and off-the-wall script. It defies categorisation, both front and back. First prize for a back which undulates like the ripples in a pond! It is reminiscent of a board stamped with 'Jordan's Woodworks' owned by Marie. (See the 'Recipes' section for her board presenting a super sourdough.)

'Sweet is the Bread of Contentment'. Loquacious, a motto guarding against excess at mealtimes. The overall effect is of elongated lettering, squeezed due to the length of the motto. The 'S' leans noticeably to the left, but the other letters follow the radial perspective.

'Sweet is the Bread of Contentment', sycamore, circa 1880, 13 inches.

'Eat thy Bread with Thankfulness' (1), bread dish, stoneware, 10 x 13 inches.

'Eat thy Bread with Thankfulness' (2), bread dish, majolica, 13 x 11 inches.

'Eat thy Bread with Thankfulness' (1). The motto is giving with one hand, but there is a moralising sting in the tail. In the shape of a bread-basket, the ends are decorated with bunches of wheat.

'Eat thy Bread with Thankfulness' (2). A majolica serving dish with a fresh water fish, possibly a tench, lying on a bed of textured cabbage. The symbolism of the Loaves and Fishes story must explain this choice of motif. And yet the manufacturer seems to have let the fish takeover and has a strange idea of what looks appetising.

'Where Reason Rules, the Appetite Obeys'. Despite its wheaty lushness, this is a warning that comfort-eating and excess will not be tolerated. The dish is identified as being dedicated to bread with its radiating wheat-burst. The Gothic capitals are backed by a basket pattern and wheat, again alluding to the ancient concept of the bread basket. The painter was clearly compensating for the mean wording!

'Where Reason Rules, the Appetite Obeys', porcelain, 13 x 10 ½ inches.

3. Marriage

Boards also became very popular wedding gifts, almost standard kit for the bride's trousseau. Wing does not have an off-the-peg Wedding Board in 1886, but in his later catalogue, two versions appear, suggesting this may have trended around the 1890s onwards. See the Wing section. There are some other examples in the collection, some lavish, some simple, to mark the momentous occasion.

The J.G.S. Wedding Board. A firm favourite among our guests, this wedding board has a joyous stubby plumpness about the wheat. There is a degree of stylisation about both the wheat and flowers. The lettering is also quite sophisticated in the high Gothic style, possibly copied out of a lettering book. The fletching on the 'J' stem and flamboyant loopings on the 'J' and 'S' terminals are ambitious. The bumpy paving effect in the centre is an attempt to create a basket pattern where the horizontals appear to weave under and over the perpendicular strands. This pattern is found to better effect in a number of pieces in the 'Artists in Wood' section. This board was clearly cherished on a sideboard or a wall, as the pattern shows little sign of wear front or back. The couple may have cut the wedding cake on it but little else. Convention has it that the groom's initial appears on the left, so the 'S' most likely refers to the groom's surname.

'J.G.S.', Wedding board, circa 1800, sycamore, 11 ½ inches.

'**J. S. W. March 1898**'. Commemorating a union, this basic board is another home-made love gift. Most of the use is on the underside, suggesting S took care to preserve the carving, a sign of mutual respect. Prince Albert was a great patron of the arts and encouraged the public to take up woodworking as a pastime. He initiated competitions for amateurs with medals and monetary rewards. This board has found its niche because it is dated March 1898, the lettering and numbers cautious and well-shaped, with some uncertain on their feet. This board, when compared to the previous board, highlights the spectrum of wealth and poverty at the time.

Despite looking so simple, it would still have required a good eight hours for an amateur to make it – probably in bad light with a poorly honed tool, during the young man's scant free time. And carving is a risky business at the best of times. Peter Benson, in his *Whittling Handbook*, recommends a cut-proof glove and leather apron. Nonetheless, plasters should be at the ready, he warns, as injuries go with the territory. On a more mystical note, whittling a breadboard for one's best-beloved is a beautiful example of Yin and Yang: their makers were mostly men and their users mostly women.

'J.S.W. March 1898', wedding board, sycamore, 12 inches.

'A.S.B. Cowes 1906', oil paint on sycamore, varnish, 11 inches.

'A.S.B. Cowes 1906'. The escutcheon bears the couple's initials, painted in italics, rather than carved, and the same goes for the date and place of their wedding, in pride of place between the ears of wheat. The change in texture between the wheat ears indicates that the board was originally deep-carved with the word 'Bread' (as the gap is short) but it was removed, rather inexpertly, by the groom, to personalise it himself. This board was not used for cutting on: it was a plaque for the wall, with an old hook and string still in evidence on the reverse. Bramhall noted that often the wives of the carvers did the painting, but this bouquet of sunflowers, still a popular wedding theme, may have been the work of the bride. Sunflowers are a joyful, optimistic colour and symbolise loyalty and longevity.

The Masson's Wedding. The custom was still very much alive in the 1950s. Much admired for its fretwork, this is the only plywood breadboard in the collection. The maker had to use plywood to create the airy feeling, as one piece of wood would have split. With plywood, thin slices of wood are layered together with

'Mr & Mrs I. H. Masson, Bread Board', birch ply, circa 1950, 12 inches.

the grain at right-angles, making for great strength even when thin. It is a joyous board, the letters tottering and staggering like inebriated wedding guests. It was never used, so it may not have met with the approval of the bride. It also feels quite delicate, with a small cutting area, and may have only been used for 'best'.

House-warming. As society changed and young men and women moved out before they married, boards became nesting presents, confirmed by anecdotes from our guests. Georgina moved into her very first flat off Northcote Road, Wandsworth, in November 1965 ('It was a slum, which was why I could afford it…'). To start her off in life, she had been given 'one double bed, one corkscrew, one tin opener and this breadboard. In that order'. It is double-sided. Her mum realised she had nothing to cut with, so she went off to Northcote Road market and bought her a breadknife to go with. Similarly with Martin: 'I bought it when I bought my own house. I liked that it was practical and caught all the crumbs in the removable tray.'

'Bermondsey 1937'. We will never know for sure what community celebration

'Bermondsey 1937', sycamore, 12 inches.

prompted the making of this board. The Coronation of George VI was a likely reason, as the collection includes other royal memorabilia with '1937' on and in a similar style. Two years before the Second World War, it was in uncertain times and maybe a couple thought the best way to keep in touch was to get married. Or was it a victory trophy made by a Labour councillor when they won all 54 seats? There's another colourful theory; celebrating the victorious routing of local fascists, as recounted by Michael Collins in *The Likes of Us*:

When Oswald Mosley's 'blackshirts' – whose headquarters were in the Walworth Road – marched to the Elephant & Castle and into Bermondsey in 1937 singing the *Horst Wessel Lied* and the hymn of Mussolini's fascist party, they were confronted by communists singing the *Red Flag*. But all these voices were drowned by the collective renditions of *Rule Britannia* and *Land of Hope and Glory* from the majority of those living nearby who had turned out on the streets. The march was diverted because the inhabitants had barricaded the streets with barrows and a water tank from a nearby factory. Eggs, door knobs, shoes, stones and oranges were tossed over the barricades at Oswald's army.

Faith in God

i. Judaism

The breadboard has a very powerful connection with the rituals of Sabbath. It is the respectful platform on which to present God's bounty and give thanks as a family and community. Practising Jews still continue this tradition on a Friday evening, minutes before sundown, when Sabbath begins. It is marked, amongst other things, by a blessing, 'Blessed are You, King of the Universe, Who brings forth bread from the earth', after which the bread is broken. Sabbath is a day of rest when equipment such as knives should not be used. The motto on the knife reads, rather confusingly, 'Holy Sabbath'. Ella, a museum visitor, explained that the knife can be used by some less strict traditions for cutting the bread.

Jerusalem board, silver plate and olive wood, circa 1960, 12 ¼ inches, with the words in Hebrew 'Jerusalem' and 'Who brings forth bread from the earth'.

Jerusalem Boards. Naomi, another visitor, recognised the decoration on this board as 'Damascene', probably made by Syrian Jews from Damascus who had fled to Israel in the 1950s. The metal workers punched the pattern in with many different shaped stipples. The insert is of olive wood, cut into small rectangular blocks and glued end-grain to create an eye-catching mosaic effect. The knife was separate. The end of the handle is marked 'Made in Israel, Bier, Stirling', with a pawn mark, 'J/9/5'. It is 13 inches long and the steel blade has the logo of a rising sun. Bier's was founded in 1950 by Jizchak Bier, a celebrated silversmith, and the firm is still in business in Israel today, offering a similar knife.

Challah board by Amy Reichert, acacia and stirling silver.
Courtesy of Amy Reichert Judaica.

Modern Challah Boards. American Judaica websites still offer a staggering variety of breadboards made of steel, marble, glass and even crystal, some resembling monumental plinths. It throws up the question: has the decline in family-focussed Christianity and a more fluid society brought about, to some extent, a decline in the use of breadboards in the UK, as we are losing the custom of a formal family meal focussed around a table. Contemporary Challah boards are also creative on a symbolic level, incorporating Biblical references, and authentic materials from the Holy Land. In Amy Reichert's beautiful piece (above), the grain in the wood is suggestive of the sand dunes the Israelites had to overcome during their 40 years wandering in the desert, and the silver salt cellar is reminiscent of an oasis.

ii. Christianity

Carrying on this tradition, the New Testament is full of references to bread as a metaphor for Jesus and his message. It continues to be considered sacred in the Act of Holy Communion, when, by eating the bread, a worshipper becomes one with Christ. In John 6:35, Jesus says: 'I am the bread of life.'

Jesus in the Cornfield, Pratt, 1851, 12 ½ inches.

Jesus in the Cornfield. This bread dish was produced for the 1851 Great Exhibition and won a medal for its groundbreaking underglaze printing. It depicts a famous moment in Matthew 12 when Jesus' disciples are plucking grains straight off the stalks on the Sabbath because they are hungry and they are criticised for 'working' and thus breaking the rules. Jesus defends them, saying 'I desire mercy, not sacrifice'. The art work is signed H. Warren. It was designed by Jesse Austin, Sculptor, in collaboration with Pratt porcelain manufacturers. It got criticised by Henry Cole as being in bad taste, to have Jesus depicted on the food surface.

The Bible is a bountiful source of mottos for breadboards, produced for customers who wished to express their faith at every meal. 'Give us this day our daily bread' and 'Our daily Bread' are more commonly occurring phrases, found in Matthew 6:11. It appears in the collection translated into many languages. (See 'Recipes' section.) There follow two memorable renditions:

'**Give Us Our Daily Bread**'. The crisp bold lettering is unusual in copying Roman typescript with delicate serifs, and is balanced with a joyous spray of foliage. The lettering ends a bit before the carver anticipated, so the spray was a useful filler.

'Give Us Our Daily Bread', sycamore 13 inches.

'**Give us this day our daily bread**'. In Chinese! One possible explanation is that it was owned by an English sinophile, merchant or missionary to China, of whom there were a great many in the 1800s-1900s, especially of the Protestant denomination. Victoria, a student of Classical Chinese literature in Hong Kong thought it was a personal translation by a Westerner studying Chinese, possibly

Classical Chinese (detail right) for 'Give us this day our daily bread', 11 inches.

the owner's, because the characters feel unnatural. The early translators wanted to convey a sense of the ancient authority of the Bible by using Confucian Chinese, as an equivalent to Latin. Comparing it with all the available variations, it is clearly inspired from versions dating between 1809 and 1889. The carving is beautifully balanced and calligraphic, suggesting a Chinese carver's work.

'Bless God the Giver'. This is not a direct quote but a distillation of James 1:17. 'Every good gift and every perfect gift is from above'. Combined with the wheat ears, it expresses simple joy that there is bread on the table. It is professional, with quirky extras such as a ribbony detail on the capital 'G'.

'Bless God the Giver', sycamore, 12 inches.

Vom Brod allein. The Germans still use these dinky *Frühstücksbrettchen* – little individual breakfast boards, in wood, porcelain or plastic – for preparing their open sandwiches for breakfast. This particular board is decorated with a humorous verse, the first part lifted from Luke 4:4, when Jesus meets the Devil after fasting for 40 days and 40 nights. The Devil asks Jesus why he is putting up with being hungry if he can make food appear. He answers: *'Der Mensch lebt nicht vom Brot allein, sondern von einem jeglichen Wort, das durch den Mund Gottes geht'* ('Man shall not live by bread alone, but by every word which comes, out of the mouth of God'). The response has been adapted into a rhyming couplet:

'*Vom Brod allein kan Man nicht leben, Es must auch Wurst und Schinken geben*', meaning 'Man cannot on bread alone live, we must have also sausage and ham with'. (!) The spelling is archaic, and predates 1908, when the German spelling reforms dictated that 'bread' should be spelled 'Brot' instead of 'Brod'.

Breakfast plate (left), German, 'Villeroy and Bosch, Dresden', Mercury ink stamp, circa 1874-1909, porcelain, 10 ½ x 5 ¾ inches. Three knives (right) with a religious theme, of boxwood and sycamore.

Three Knives

1. 'If he ask for bread will ye give him a stone'. An amusing inscription, as it is shaming the owner into being generous, and could have been a gift for stubbornly thrifty relatives. The source quotation is: 'If his son asks him for bread, will he give him a stone?' from Matthew 7:9.

2. Saint. With no distinguishing features, the carving is in the vein of apostles spoons, harking back to medieval church niches with statues of Jesus. It includes strapwork and leaves, is flattened, and was available wholesale as it is found on the blades of different cutlers.

3. Fish. A rare handle with a fish both sides, alluding to the loaves and fish story, and possibly matched a breadboard with fish on which Rosslyn sold and regretted. It went to a nunnery. The blade with GR, George V 1911-36.

Winchester Boards. Prince Albert's Christian Revival brought a flood of investment in the Anglican Church's crumbling infrastructure. The renewed interest in the Faith brought pilgrims flocking to the great old cathedral towns, where souvenirs were on sale, some derived from the ancient oak salvaged from ongoing renovations. Catering for the parallel need for advice on restoring Medieval art, a book on woodcarving recommends: 'Oak…from its hard and enduring nature, should as a rule be chosen for executing the finials or pew-heads, alms-boxes, church and Gothic works in general.' In particular: 'The wood principally used in the decorative carving of our cathedrals during the Middle Ages was the true British oak, or *Quercus robur.*' For Winchester boards see sections below on Laverty and Bramhall in 'Artists in Wood'.

'God Loveth a Cheerful Giver', alms dish, oak, 8 ¾ inches.

Alms Dishes. Luckily for the turners and carvers, churches were stocking up on beautifully carved wooden accessories also. For collecting contributions from the congregations, alms dishes were carved with guilt trips like 'God loveth a cheerful giver', an adaptation of 2 Corinthians 9:7 'because the gift comes from a heart that has been made glad', and 'Freely you have received, freely give', from Matthew 10:8. The latter is back in the possession of the clergy, at Rev'd Moy's home in Chiswick, and is being used as a candle stand.

King and Country

The royal boards form an interesting snapshot of carving trends, spanning fifty-four years of jubilees and coronations.

Victoria: 1887 and 1897. The five carved during Victoria's reign are all different and a joyous celebration of skill and monarchy.

'Jubilee of our Empress Queen'. This board is gracefully carved in Old English text. It is not possible to date exactly, but it may be referring to Victoria's 40th year on the throne, which coincided with Prime Minister Disraeli proclaiming Queen Victoria Empress of India, as of 1 January 1877. Its incised Gothic lettering is very professional.

'British Jubilee 1887'. This board commemorates Victoria's Golden Jubilee

'Jubilee of our Empress Queen', circa 1880s, sycamore, 12 ½ inches.

'British Jubilee 1887', sycamore, 12 inches.

on her 50th anniversary as queen. It is embellished with the floral badges of the United Kingdom: the Tudor rose of England, the thistle of Scotland and the shamrock of Ireland. The leek of Wales is not included as Wales was considered a Principality, the domain of a Prince – the Prince of Wales – not a country. Another example can be found at the Somerset Rural Life Museum near Glastonbury. It is carved with great finesse.

'George V' bread plate, sycamore, 10 ¾ inches.

'Coronation 1937', bread plate, remains of red staining, sycamore, 10 inches.

'1837 V.R. 1897'. This board welcomes Victoria's Diamond Jubilee in letters shaped like twigs with flowers, V.R. standing for *Victoria Regina*. The border is filled with generously carved wheat ears and veined leaves, possibly by an amateur. The initials 'W.F.' are visible on the upper side, and the reverse is engraved 'Highfield Park W.F.', suggesting W.F. is possibly the maker. Research has not been able to pinpoint W.F.'s identity.

George V, 1911. The collection does not have a commemorative board for Edward VII's coronation in 1901, but picks up with that of George V, which presents a complete contrast to the Victorian boards above. It is a smaller 'bread plate', which would have fitted into the plate rack above the sink. The square lettering was available from the 1880s, but came into fashion at the beginning of the 20th century, as Gothic flamboyance and Renaissance overload were going out of style.

'**Coronation 1937.**' Another 'bread plate', it welcomes George VI to the throne after the shockingly messy abdication of his brother Edward VIII. George VI's coronation day was originally intended for Edward VIII, which may explain why the motto remains non-committal about naming the King, for fear of backing the wrong horse. The basic carving may also be evidence of a chronic skills shortage caused by the bloodshed of the First World War. Its small size may have been connected to cautious consumer spending, as war was again looming. However, there were celebrations and street parties in some quarters, and these boards may have been made or bought to decorate the trestle tables arranged down the street.

There may have been many factors driving the change of taste. Society was

'1837 V.R. 1897', sycamore, 13 inches.

in flux with socialism and communism fighting for better wages, thus driving up labour costs. Bauhaus was becoming fashionable, with plain clean lines. Servants were becoming a thing of the past, meaning the mistress of the house would have wanted more practical tableware which was easy to clean. Bacteria had been discovered and the push for cleanliness would not have favoured deep-cut carving with endless cavities to disinfect. Finally, Fascism was rearming an ever more belligerent Germany, causing economic uncertainty. It may be a coincidence, but breadboards celebrating the two Kings were definitely more understated than those celebrating the Queens!

'Long Life and Happiness', Coronation Board for Queen Elizabeth II, 1953, Bramhall, Sheffield, sycamore, 12 inches.

'**Long Life and Happiness ER June 2 1953**'. This board signals a sea-change; that the country wanted to party again at the coronation of Queen Elizabeth II after the horrors of the Second World War. Despite the bombsites everywhere, there was talk of a 'New Elizabethan Age'. The carving is rich, traditional and intricate, the motto joyful and usually seen in the context of wedding salutations. Three examples are known which are identical and were made by Bramhall, one of the few companies left producing boards of quality by the 1950s. (See the 'Bramhall' section.) Queen Elizabeth has indeed had a long, eventful life and we wish her continued good health and happiness in the years to come.

'**Cymru am byth MDCCCXCIX**'. This 12-inch sycamore board (below) is inscribed with the patriotic Welsh motto '*Cymru am byth*' which translates as 'Wales for Ever'. It may have been inspired by the upsurge in fighting spirit at the start of the Boer War in 1899. The Roman numerals give it added formality and importance, while the capital letters make it sound like a battle cry.

'Nemo me impune lacessit', board and matching butter dish, sycamore,
11 ½ inches and 7 ½ inches, reproduction glass insert.

'Nemo me impune lacessit'. For those with an allegiance to the Kings of Scotland, a breadboard and butter dish with the rallying cry *'Nemo me impune lacessit'* would have hit the spot. Often translated into the Scots *'Wha duar meddle wi me'* (in Scottish Gaelic *'Cha togar m' fhearg gun dìoladh'*), it is loosely translated as 'No one can harm me with impunity', rather like the thistle. The motto was added to the arms of the King of Scotland during the reign of Charles II. A Wing board, it was made to order as it does not appear in the catalogue, but bears his signature bobbly serifs.

Royal Bread Knives

1. Coronation May 1937, a standard bread knife, the blade etched with GR & ER, surmounted by a crown, plastic handle, Wade and Butcher, Sheffield.
2. Diamond Jubilee butter knife, bone handled, 1837-1897, marked 'Reg'd', with a Portrait of the Queen with Rose, Thistle and Shamrock.
3. Diamond Jubilee bread knife, ribbons with flowers peeping out, square lettering, boxwood.
4. Four Thistles bread knife. A more economy model for the Scottish market, in the naive style, boxwood.
5. Scotland, with a bold thistle and wheat on the reverse, ivory, Joseph Rodgers blade, VR, registration mark on the blade.
6. Prince of Wales feathers which take up nearly half the handle, the Rose Thistle and Shamrock smaller scale, possibly for the Welsh market, boxwood handle.

Expressions of Taste

So far we have seen the potential for breadboards to boost status and broadcast beliefs. This third section gives an insight into how they represent our taste in art, our consumer habits and our love of Nature.

Art: Victorian Period

The Victorians were rapacious in their plundering of the world and the contemporary artistic response was to use styles both European and from further afield to create new trends. 'Victorian' typically meant a sensory overload as Gothic jostled with Renaissance, Arts and Crafts, Moorism, Japonisme and so on.

A) RENAISSANCE STYLE

The century started with a dignified continuation of the Renaissance. William Gibbs Rogers, a preeminent carver, spearheaded a renewed demand for Renaissance woodcarving, in the form of Gibbons-inspired creations (see 'Artists in Wood' for more). The following breadboards and knife handles are in the Renaissance style, showing great skill in the naturalistic depiction of the motifs.

'MCN', 1885 Wedding board, maple, 13 ¼ inches.

MCN 1885 Wedding board. Behold a masterpiece. It is absolutely exquisitely done in maple, which is harder than sycamore and heavier. A wedding board, the peas bulging in the pods may be symbolic of a large healthy family. This is one of only three examples of the motif in the collection. The harvest theme of wheat, barley and peapods surrounded by delicate tendrils and foliage is a very Gibbons touch. The sweetcorn was not known to Gibbons, giving this piece a contemporary twist. The carving is extremely sophisticated: note the superbly uniform beads with no visible beginning or end, the minutely carved corn hulls and individual barley whiskers ('awns'). Tom Samuel observed that every bead in the beading takes five minutes – for an experienced carver. The carver may have worked for stately homes producing pendants, panelling, staircases and picture frames. The ink inscription on the reverse reads: 'Alexr Douglas, Woodcarver, 169 Fountainbridge, Edinburgh, 26th December 1885', though he was not found in any directories of the period. The reverse was covered in baize originally, which preserved the inscription. Fountainbridge was a burgeoning mixture of working class tenements and industry near the Union Canal and was inhabited by a rapidly changing assortment of tradesmen.

The Snail Platter. The carving on this sycamore board (below) is masterful; it is possibly an exhibition piece as it looks unused. The design is without beginning

or end, is naturalistic and is a burst of wheat and wild flowers. The snail is left proud of the flowers, suggesting a considerable wastage of wood, or the carver may have left the blank wedge-shaped. The snail is reminiscent of one on a limewood sculpture, 'Golden Plover', winner of a Prize Medal at the Paris Exposition of 1855, by Thomas Wilkinson Wallis of Louth, the very same carver who produced the platter for Alfred Lord Tennyson (see 'Status Symbols').

The Weather Board. An aberration in its scroll shape, this is in the Renaissance style. The motifs include numerous classical allusions, namely the four winds, lightning (Zeus/Jupiter), the sun (Helios/Sol), and two dolphins (Poseidon/Neptune).

The Weather board, oak, early 20th century, 14 x 12 inches.

Early Bread Knives. The bread knife handle began as a traditional 18th century pattern for any multi-purpose kitchen knife, so cutlers were creating a seemingly new line but without any major innovations. The question of why clients wanted to buy a knife devoted to bread remains, but we can speculate it started with the Corn Laws bumping up the price of bread. This then drove the need to show it off nicely. We cannot be sure which came first, the breadboard or bread knife, but these knives make one wonder if the knife didn't come first, and then clients wanted to upgrade their plain old chopping boards. Possibly, cutting bread had been a kitchen job, but once bread became expensive, it might have been brought front-of-house to be on show, and thus more elegant presentation was required.

Focussing on Handles. Apart from dating purposes, we do not give a guide to blade makers, except when the stamp is indicating a known carver, or a significant date or location. Blades are peripheral to the carving process, as the handles were sold loose wholesale and retail. Blade stamps are an unreliable indication even of the cutler, as cutlers would stamp the customer's name if he bought over 100 pieces, and generally give no indication of the handle maker.

A selection of Mappin bread knives, boxwood and ivory handles, 1800-1900s.

Mappin Brothers Knives. This selection mimics the classical traditions promoted by Gibbons, showing styles in art pre-existing bread knives, which were applied to this new popular domestic item. In the Great Exhibition of 1851, Mappin Brothers were exhibiting: 'Carved-wood bread-platters with suitable designs and mottos. Bread knives, with carved and fluted ivory and wood handles'. One such fluted handle can be seen in the photograph, although a later piece, stamped

Mappin & Webb, proving that the line was a popular one. A Sheffield-based company of unstinting high quality, they were also bringing an exquisite sense of taste to the bread knife craze, in competition with the Summerly/Rodgers collaboration. See 'Artists in Wood' for more.

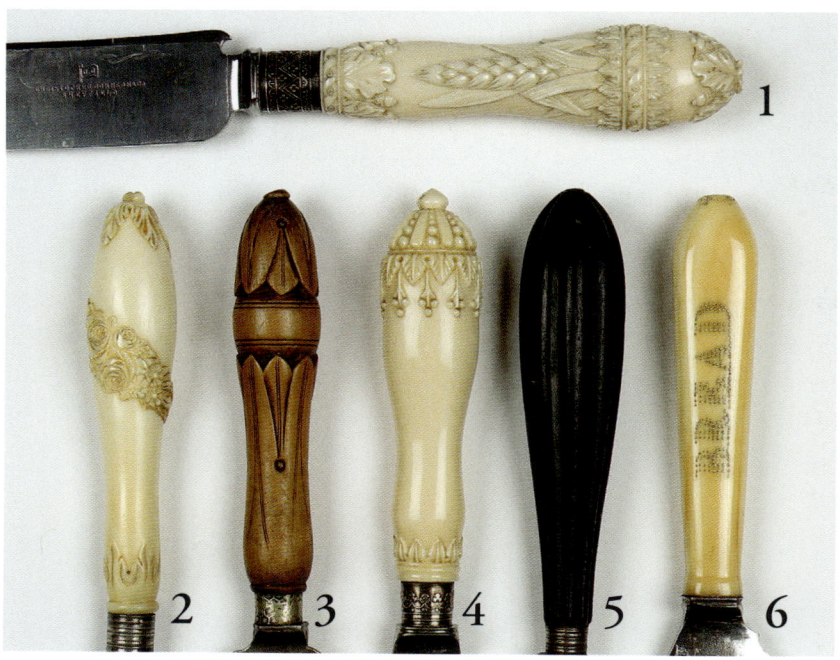

Bread knives with Renaissance-style handles (above).

1. A high Victorian handle, showing an obsession with ornament, the lavishness due to the carver's incorporating all styles of decoration in one go. We see the classical mouldings have been joined by acorns and wheat, as bread knives developed a recognisable style of their own. Later Victorian bread knives dispensed with the word 'Bread' as everyone recognised the wheat-symbol. A later blade has been added.

2. A miniaturisation of a Gibbons pendant, with an acanthus tip, ivory.

3. Neo-Classical style boxwood handle, the motif called water leaf and husk, a late 18th century style.

4. An ivory handle carved in the Regency style, a fair example of an earlier style being used to fuel the new bread knife craze.

5. A reeded bog-wood handle. A great industry was burgeoning in Ireland, with a stand at the Great Exhibition. They made good tourist souvenirs, and once dried, became very dense and hard. Early 19th century.

6. A bone handle with 'BREAD' drilled and filled with brass wire, probably the earliest form of specialised bread knife.

Bread knives made of exotic materials (above)

1. An antelope horn handle with silver enrichments, this piece harks back to the taste for using hunting trophies such as deer antler in cutlery. It brings an exotic twist with a novelty African species. The ripples in the horn were perfect for gripping, the natural curve creating a pistol-grip effect, by Mappin Bros.

2. A home-grown cow-horn handle, and a very common shape in the 18th century. Only the tip of a cow horn is solid, then it goes hollow, so cutlers could only make a short handle from a horn. The blade is stamped Bread Knife.

3. A green stained ivory handle, more used in the 18th century. It could possibly be woolly mammoth tusk, as it is an unattractive greyish colour in its natural state, and could take the stain because it is porous, unlike fresh ivory. On the blade: George Lowcock, 38 Cornhill, (1839-50). The 'BREAD' stamp, in capitals on the diagonal is early.

4. A 19th century copy of an 18th century pistol grip-style handle, so popular that sometimes makers mounted old ones onto new blades, silver.

5. An agate stone handle of superb quality, attractively banded, which has survived unbroken. This is a huge achievement, given that agate is very delicate and brittle. This could be the cream of the output of that period, with an early stainless steel blade, Sheffield, 1913.

Bread knives showing old styles in new materials (above)

1. The parian handle is a version of a parasol handle designed by Strudwick in 1849, and it is uncomfortable to hold horizontally. It is a better design for holding vertically as the wide end would be easy to grasp. Post 1849.

2. The same Strudwick parasol handle design, applied to a bread knife, but this time in silver plate. These were made in large quantities.

3. This handle is made from some form of early plastic material. These would have been stamped out in vast quantities, as cutlers were businessmen looking for a cheaper solution to carving. The handle is decorated with oak leaves and acorns. The blade is stamped GR (George V).

4. Another handle of a similar material, decorated with a birds and leaves design. The blade is stamped VR.

5. Another handle of early plastic material. With a wheat and flower design, and a Joseph Rodgers blade, stamped VR. It is likely that this design was particular to Rodgers, as the great cutlers wished to be known for their unique lines.

B) GOTHIC REVIVAL

Spurred on by Barry's plans for an all new Houses of Parliament, Neo-Gothic was also a prominent trend through the Victorian era. There follows a selection of Gothic contributions from the collection. It seems extraordinary now, but the most famous designers, artists and retailers of their age did not feel it below themselves to produce and supply top-of-the-range bread-platters and knives. A few notable examples of bread-platters appear here, and many Neo-Gothic bread knife handles can be seen across the book, recognisable by their Gothic lettering and miniaturised church ornamentation.

Pugin. Minton collaborated with Pugin to bring an old encaustic tile technique associated with flooring, to the table. Pugin found time to design his own bread-platter for the Great Exhibition while in the middle of managing the interiors of the Houses of Parliament. Minton was still producing these platters, in this different colour way in 1875, of which one example is held at the Fitzwilliam.

Minton's Bread Tray, designed by Pugin, 1851, earthenware, 13 ¾ inches.

c) Other Styles

After the Gothic Revival, the end of the 1800s saw a quick succession of styles blossoming and fading. Breadboard companies saw the benefit of keeping abreast of these developments as trendy consumers upgraded.

Moorish

One of the many styles that the Victorians dabbled in, it was encouraged by William Morris. This board is inspired by Islamic geometry, expressed with fine chip carving, and delicately incised lines.

Moorish board, sycamore, 12 inches.

Arts and Crafts

Thompson Octagon. Robert Thompson began his joiner career in the 1920s, and set up his own company as a cottage industry, following the tenets of the Arts and Crafts movement which encouraged the artist to leave a visible footprint. Known as the 'Mouseman', his creations are characterised by visible tool marks and simple unadorned shapes. The mouse is symbolic and harks back to his early days after the war when he was 'as poor as a church mouse', and gives some character to the basic shape. Thompson follows a popular and successful formula, with the mouse as a subtle signature. Each mouse is unique to a carver, and the workshop dated this one to the 1950s. The cutting surface is inscribed with two lines of a mystical Christian poem entitled 'Imminence' by Evelyn Underhill, relating to small furry creatures.

Thompson octagon, 1950s, oak, 12 x 8 inches.

Inky Board and Butterdish. This rare matching pair of breadboard and butter dish was reunited recently, and definitely came from the same house because the hanging holes are identical. Their pristine condition is thanks to having been hung on a wall as art. Deeply cut, the harvest fare is carved on a larger scale than usual, the magnification giving them an exuberance. Their link to A&C is the staining of the wood with blue-black ink, an idea promoted by Philip Webb, the architect and friend of William Morris. The distinctive ribbon gathering the corn is found on three other boards in the collection and is an example of a carver's signature which we cannot attribute. (See the 'Welcome' board in the 'Introduction').

Inky board and butter dish, sycamore, 12 and 9 ½ inches.

Honesty. This pattern (below) on a 12 ½ inch sycamore board was possibly inspired by William Morris who popularised the use of honesty in his designs, and appears on three known examples.

Art Nouveau

At the turn of the 1900s, new styles developed and breadboards kept apace.

Lily Pad Cheese Board. This board celebrates pure art nouveau, with its lily pads and tendrils, and its subtle blending of round and square forms. As the lily-pads occur in each corner, less wood would have been wasted. It would have been hard work gouging out by hand between the lily pads because the lathe could not be used. Cheese boards have a deep, flat-bottomed gully for the dome. Crumb grooves are many shapes and sizes.

Lily pad cheese board, sycamore, 13 ½ inches.

HOK Board. An earlier Art Nouveau silverplated dish has been married up with a sycamore liner that was originally plain, but carved at a later date in the Vienna Secessionist style, and bears the monogram HOK. It possibly stands for Hermann Obrist Kunst (1863-1927), although he specialised in textiles.

HOK board, silver plate and sycamore, 12 inches.

Oval with Tendrils. A typical Art Nouveau look, the stems or leaves are curving back over themselves.

Oval with tendrils, sycamore, 12 x 10 inches.

'**Bread 1920**'. With very expressive, 3-D lettering, this is reminiscent of the curves of Hector Guimard, each letter with varying heights. It is heavy and thick, with no holes in the back which means the maker had the luxury of taking time on both the original design and making phases.

'Bread 1920', sycamore, 12 inches, 1 ¼ inches deep.

Art Deco

Thistle & Rose Oval. Used as a breadboard, this was possibly carved in England for the French market, where bread was presented pre-cut on dishes or in baskets. The motifs are simple with plain empty spaces, giving it a clean, uncluttered look.

Off-centre Leaves. The stylised foliage is unique in its asymmetry, a playful experiment in bringing the Art Deco style to breadboards in an eye-catching way. The carver was thinking outside the box. The motion of the lathe tends to force the artist to think symmetrically. There is still a pleasing balance, with a concentrated splash of decoration.

Off-centre leaves, sycamore, 12 inches.

Tourism and Travel

As ever, entrepreneurs, turners and carvers saw the potential for breadboards as an advertising vehicle, and threw themselves into juicy contracts supplying towns, resorts, bakers, millers and retailers. There follows a selection of boards which provided a happy reminder for our parents, grandparents and great-grandparents of where they holidayed, what they liked eating, and what they loved in nature.

Winchester. Already in the 1880s, Winchester was making the most of the tourist trade. See Laverty and Bramhall for carved goods. But other articles were being produced by local artists and silversmiths.

Pasted Images. In 1915, stick-on images were being applied to the salvaged wood, a cheaper alternative to carving. Mr G Green Smith, once a resident of Winchester, wrote in *Notes and Queries* of 1915: 'I bought, at a stall outside its glorious old cathedral, a little square tablet of wood, represented to me as being cut out of a piece of wood removed of necessity from the edifice during restorative work. On the front of the little tablet was pasted an exceedingly neat and well-executed coloured cut representing the Trusty Servant, the colours copied, I believe, from the original painting…'

F.J. Ross, Silversmiths. Aside from the Cathedral shop and Laverty's gallery, the souvenir trade included a number of retailers specialising in different materials. Jacob & Ross, Silversmiths, appear in 1884, as 'manufacturers of St. Cross Ornaments' and Ross continued on into the 1930s at least. Two plain square tablets of oak by Frederick J Ross & Sons, at 43-44 High St, Winchester, are embellished with a silver inlay, one of the Trusty Servant and the second of the cross of St Cross. Both of ancient oak, they are reminiscent of medieval trenchers, many of which didn't have a depression. They were used as breadboards, as there is no evidence of fork prong holes, only sawing.

Trusty Trencher, silver inlay on oak, hallmarked 1938, 9 x 9 inches

St Cross trencher, silver inlay on oak, Chester, 1931, 11 x 11 inches

From Brighton. This board was likely made by Bramhall, the unique feature being its anchor and a maritime theme carried into the rope-effect border.

'From Brighton', sycamore, 12 inches.

Assorted tableware purchased as souvenirs from seaside resorts.

Wolverhampton. Very shallowly carved with the unofficial arms of the city, there are signs of staining on the back to make the carving more pronounced, with a sanding to finish off. It has been used, despite cutting on the arms. There is quite a story behind this 'unofficial' coat of arms.

Wolverhampton was recognised as a Borough in 1848 and granted a Charter which would have entitled it to a coat of arms. However George Thorneycroft, a wealthy ironmaster and the first Mayor, did not receive one from the College of Arms. The latter has, regrettably, not contributed any insights into the circumstances.

So Alfred Hall Browne, Master Extraordinary in the High Court of Chancery, and a local Wolverhampton solicitor, created an unofficial coat of arms, presumably at the request of Mayor Thorneycroft. The elements all related to Wolverhampton's heritage and aimed to crystallise all that was noble or noteworthy.

Wolverhampton, sycamore, worm damaged, 12 inches.

Most remarkable amongst these is the stone column appearing in the centre of the middle shield. It depicts a historic relic of 'Wulfrun-hamptun', dating possibly from Saxon times, and is still standing today in the main church of St.

Peter's. The V&A considered it precious enough to have a wax cast made in 1880 (V&A 1880-117).

Using a coat of arms without authorisation was not unknown, so the 'original' design appeared throughout the Borough on buildings of the period, and can still be seen on a bridge of 1879 over the canal at the Black Country Living Museum. Forty-five years later, and a year after Browne's death, his creation was being publicly mocked by a fellow lawyer, Arthur Charles Fox-Davies in *A Book of Public Arms* (1894). He pours scorn on the 'bogus escutcheon' in his section on Wolverhampton, criticising such heraldry 'affected by ignorant amateurs' as being 'too good a joke to be omitted'.

At the end of the section Fox-Davies delivers the final punch: 'There is a slang name we have for Wolverhampton down in the Midlands. The display affected in the foregoing is much in keeping therewith.' The College of Arms did produce an official insignia in 1898, on the occasion of the 50th anniversary of the Borough, but the old version is still preferred by fans of Wolverhampton Wanderers FC.

The Jungfrau, Switzerland. The British became very enamoured of hiking in the Swiss Alps and bought many locally carved wooden items. The breadboard craze surely influenced the Swiss to create breadboard-shaped goods with a Swiss twist. Although purely decorative, this very delicately painted wall-platter, is framed with high relief carving of Edelweiss and sweet gentian, which is also found around many breadboards. A guest to the museum who was born in Switzerland explained how Edelweiss used to be a love token for a young man to offer to his sweetheart. But the flower grows in very inaccessible places and led to several tragic deaths, causing the custom to fall out of favour.

'Jungfrau' dish, 11 ½ inches.

124

The Antarctic. Certainly the most far-flung. Not exactly tourism, but absolutely ticking the 'adventure' box, Robert Falcon Scott (1868-1912) took a breadboard with him to the Antarctic. Here it is, presenting their bread in a rather posed way, on the return of Dr Wilson, Lt Bowers and Apsley Cherry-Garrard from Cape Crozier, 1 August 1911. Scott wrote: 'They looked more weatherworn than anyone I have yet seen. Their faces were scarred and wrinkled, their eyes dull… That men should wander forth in the depth of the Polar night to face the most dismal cold and the fiercest gales in darkness is something new; that they should have persisted in this effort in spite of every adversity for five full weeks is heroic. It makes a tale for our generation which I hope may not be lost in the telling.' After post-morteming the journey, the only suggestion was an additional cup of cocoa in the evenings.

Not an obvious piece of kit for the contemporary Antarctic explorer, it did come in handy for more than just cutting bread on. The board is no longer to be found among the Scott Polar Research Institute collection, nor is it in the Antarctic Heritage Trust (AHT), Christchurch, New Zealand, where many of the remaining items from the hut have been stored. Diana Pope in Wellington, NZ, kindly tracked down Lizzie Meek of the AHT who has painstakingly catalogued every object and suggested that 'it is highly likely it got burnt on the stove for fuel by the Ross Sea Party, as it is a very conveniently stove-sized piece of wood, and they ran out of coal and had to switch to using other materials including seal blubber.'

British Antarctic Expedition 1910-13, taken by Herbert Ponting. Getty Images.

Advertising and Promotion

Many companies advertised themselves by offering 'token' boards and knives, where customers were incentivised to collect a certain number of tokens in order to earn a 'freebee'.

Artox, the Millers. Appleyards were Millers and Corn Merchants in Rotherham from 1855, and traded under the name 'Artox'. They specialised in wholemeal flour which gained a reputation for unadulterated high quality and its health giving properties. Their slogans were 'The outcome of the finest wheat', and 'The Wheat, the whole Wheat and nothing but the Wheat'. The Food Adulteration Acts of the 1860s put the onus on bakers to clean up their bread, and customers became more discerning.

The benefits of Artox, 'with every whit of the wheat', were still being extolled in 'Constipation and the pursuit of Health in Modern Society' in 1942, in which the author goes as far as to say: 'the whiter your bread, the sooner you're dead'.

'Artox' board and knife, nicely lettered board, probably Bramhall, 1920-30s, the blade also stamped with the Artox brand, sycamore, 11 ½ inches.

Allinson, the Millers. Allinson flour also prided itself on its health benefits. 'A Very Modern Victorian', Dr. Thomas R. Allinson 'was an energetic campaigner for the benefits of wholemeal'. Born in 1858, he trained as a doctor at Edinburgh and was active during the last twenty years of the 1800s, bringing awareness to the medical community, bakers and consumers of England that diet was more fundamental to maintaining good health than bottles of medicine. He states: 'It is also an ascertained fact that persons who eat white bread are more inveterate drinkers, smokers and tea drinkers than those who live on Wholemeal bread'. He avoided all stimulants such as alcohol and tea. 'If a law could be passed forbidding the separation of the bran from the fine flour,' he mused, 'it would add very greatly to the health and wealth of our nation, and lessen considerably the receipts of the publican, tobacconist, chemist, doctor and undertaker.' His unguarded comments got him struck off the BMA which he fought in the courts. 'Health without Medicine' was his motto!

Suspicious of millers and bakers, he set up his own mill in Bethnal Green, East London in 1892, using traditional grinding methods 'without the sacrifice of a particle of the food value of the wheat'. The tone of the publicity materials was respectful and caring, which is how his son described him. He vetted bakers and certified them as able to use his flour, performing spot checks to ensure quality, and organised bakers' competitions. Where his patients had no Allinson-

'Allinson bread' (10 ¾ inches) and knives, 1920-30s, one knife is etched with the words 'Use Allinson Wholemeal'.

approved baker nearby, he provided bags of his flour for them to bake at home. The wholemeal revival took off through the 1920s, encouraged by mainstream media and his business expanded to two more mills. Wholemeal has been promoted as the healthier option ever since.

Hovis goods, including a silver plaque for the winner's shields, a lead baker's cart set, a doll's loaf, and a baking tin.

Hovis, the Millers. Hovis benefited from the momentum created by Artox and Dr Allinson's findings and became a market leader in supplying wholemeal flour to bakeries, containing their patented wheat-germ which improved the shelf-life of their bread. They led an assertive advertising campaign to win over bakers to their product, running competitions with important prizes including polished oak shields embellished with Stirling silver Hovis plaques, a silver scroll having the winner's name engraved on it. First prize in the Competition Finals in London 1900-1910 was 'a horse and Baker's delivery van, complete with harness'. Cigarette cases and other fancy goods were offered as 'promotional incentives' to baker customers.

Consumers were also courted with assertions about how Hovis was the only way to keep good health. Using Dr Allinson's wording, Hovis was promoted with its 'nitrogenous and flesh-forming bodies', which were 'absolutely necessary for all growing children'. Hovis-branded toys for dolls' houses and miniature lead baker's barrows were building a familiarity among the younger generation. Much was made of the Queen eating Hovis.

They were aiming for the dominant market share. A sales conference agenda of 1905 makes time for 'suggestions for the better fighting of this rivalry'. One advertisement shows a wolf snarling and the warning; 'The Public are Cautioned against accepting from Bakers spurious imitations of "HOVIS", which, having met with such unprecedented success, is being copied in many instances as closely as can be done without risk.' They kept a keen eye on their bakers: 'Bakers recommending any other bread in the place of "Hovis" do so for their own profit. Beware!' They also routinely encouraged consumers to write in to them if loaves were unsatisfactory, including the loaf in question, all costs defrayed, as a form of external quality control.

Mr Dunkley, Display and Design Executive for Rank Hovis in 1981 wrote: 'One word of warning, if you are collecting bread boards, I do recall (in 1953) issuing an elaborate window display unit which had, attached to a sloping back panel, a real Hovis breadboard. This board had two wooden spikes let into the centre of the board on which a Hovis loaf could be securely pronged. I have little doubt that a number of these found their way into general use but can be identified by the sawn-off spikes appearing as filling plugs in the centre of the board'.

He also kindly provided a copy of 'The Hovis Knife', advertised in 1901, 'This knife supersedes all other bread and cake knives. It cuts better, straighter and easier. This is due to the wave pattern edge and to the double grinding, making the edge the centre of the knife. This is how it improves on the saw-edge knife and surpasses the straight edge. Handle it and try it! That is all we ask.'

Daren Bread, the Bakers. From the 1890s to the 1930s Daren bread was a household name and rivalled Hovis – until it was bought out by them. The firm's slogan, 'Made from the life of the wheat' promoted its bread as a healthy wholemeal product, distinctive for its 'admixture of germ and rye meal'. As bread tins became widespread, bread went rectangular, but the small loaves that Daren produced could still fit on round boards that were originally designed for the cottage-loaf style.

Daren butterdish or ashtray, depicting a loaf of their bread on a breadboard with a knife, glass, 8 inches.

Fletcher's Bakery. A famous Sheffield company dating from 1895, they coined the slogan 'Better fetch a Fletcher's loaf'. Highly automated, it was bought out in 2014 and supplies white bread goods in bulk to food chains and hotels.

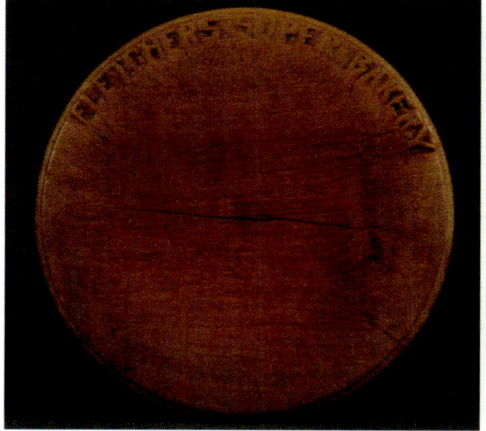 

| 'Fletchers Super Bakery', in small capitals, sycamore, 10 inches. | 'Abbott & Co. Xmas 1907', sycamore, 10 inches. |

'Abbott & Co. Xmas 1907'. There is a tradition of firms giving Christmas presents to significant business associates, and this may have been an example.

Allerton's Board and Pin. A pastry cum breadboard, with a matching rolling pin. 'Allerton's Your Daily Bread' on the board, 'Allerton's Baker's and Confectioners' on the pin. Branded with a stamp, showing score marks to line up the stamp.

Allerton's board, 13 ½ x 10 inches, and rolling pin, 17 inches, beech.

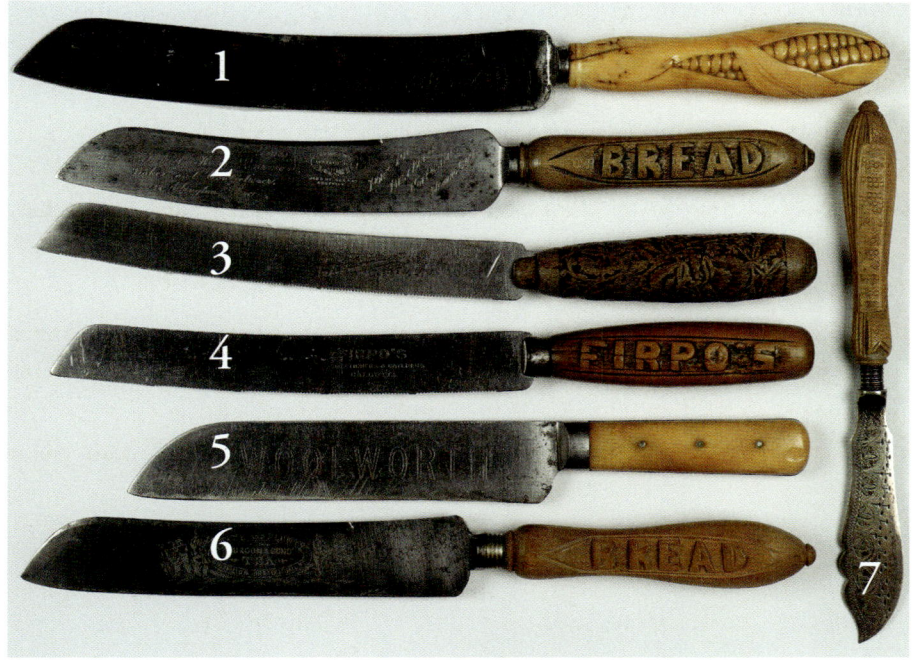

Advertising Bread Knives

1. 'Hardings Current Bread' with an ivory sweetcorn handle, possibly matched later.

2. 'BREAD' is etched on the sycamore handle, the blade inscribed with: 'Look forward to meal times and deal with H. E. Burman Baker and Confectioner, 28 Abington Grove, Pork Pies Best Bread Hot Pastries and Wedding Cakes'.

3. A bread knife with an Indian handle fixed to a Sheffield steel blade 'Vallimahomed Dattoobhai & Co. Bombay'.

4. 'FIRPO'S Confectioners and Caterers Calcutta', on the handle and the blade.

5. 'WOOLWORTHS' on the blade, with a deer antler handle.

6. 'BURGON and Sons TEA', with 'Peace and Plenty' on the blade, 'BREAD' on the handle, Sheffield.

7. 'TIP TOP TEA' butter knife, with a nicely veined handle.

Veda Bread. The company becomes newsworthy in 1913 when the *Glasgow Herald* mentions how Veda Bread has just bought 'the most attractive van in Glasgow' for speeding up deliveries, and is planning expansion to Manchester. They boasted of vast quantities of their bread being consumed on the ocean liners and of their product soon reaching as far south as the Metropolis. The advertisements from the First World War period show how companies had no qualms about guilt-tripping their customers into boosting sales. Heart-wrenching reasons were used, such as 'The ONLY Bread that reaches the Trenches Sweet and Fresh', and 'German bread is uneatable' and 'He'll welcome this memory of home – and YOU'.

The *London Gazette* of December 1920 announced they were expanding across London. The company sent this promotional 'Sample' knife to a 'Miss J. Coxhead of 94 Mayfield Road, Sanderstead, by Rail, 3.11.23', at a cost of thruppence from their new address at 17 & 17A Sheen Lane, East Sheen S.W. according to their company address label. Veda bread is much prized in Northern Ireland to this day, and is made with malted grains, where the cereal is allowed to germinate before being processed. The advertisement's logo matches that of the modern Veda Bakeries, registered in Edinburgh, Scotland.

Veda Knife in its original packaging, 1923, wood, steel, cardboard, paper.

Green and Pleasant Land

This is a personal selection by Tom and I of our favourite boards and knives depicting Mother Nature: we cannot attribute them, but the boards talk to us. The motifs fall into four categories: Landscapes, Harvest, Flowers & Fruit, and finally Woodland.

i) Landscapes

Hawthorn. Wheat and acorns and hawthorn are a rare combination. Symbolising farming, woodland and hedgerow, the carving is precise and controlled, in medium-high relief. Note the detailing down to the ridges in the foot of the twig.

Pokerwork Riverbank. A skillfully executed landscape scene, it is remarkable for its subtle details such as hazy foliage and successful perspective. The edging is more traditional pokerwork, now called pyrography.

Hawthorn, stamped 'R. Winn', the
carver, on reverse, circa 1870,
sycamore, 13 inches,

Pokerwork riverbank, signed GC
on reverse, circa 1910,
sycamore, 10 inches.

ii) Harvest

Stag and Cross Bones. With fun sweetcorn poking out, the carving is shallow, but the carver achieves good definition on the wheat the barley. He has maximised effect with minimum effort or 'roughing out'. The crest is unknown.

Hops All Round. A deeply cut, lush board, the pattern is not symmetrical or repeating. Note the small wheat ears poking out from behind.

Stag and crossbones, circa 1890,
sycamore, 12 inches.

Hops all round, circa 1860,
sycamore, 13 inches.

133

Three wheat two rye, circa 1880,
sycamore, 13 inches.

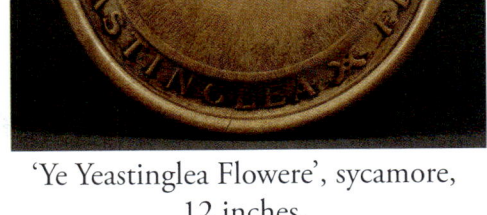

'Ye Yeastinglea Flowere', sycamore,
12 inches.

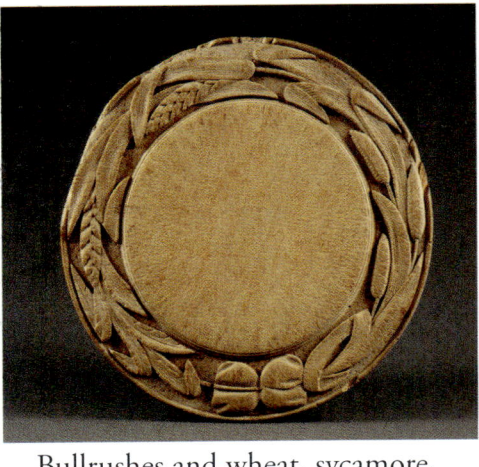

Bullrushes and wheat, sycamore,
12 inches.

Wheat basket, fruit wood,
13 inches.

Wheat and Maple. Made of very heavy wood, and thicker than an English board, this stands out for its bold carving, suggestive of North America.

Wheat and maple, possibly maple, 13 inches.	Double barley, sycamore, circa 1860, 13 inches.

Double barley. A deeply cut pattern, with great movement reinforced by the

Bullrushes and Wheat. This rare combination shows a deeply cut style with lots of energy. The two irregular circles possibly represent the bulrush roots.

Wheat Basket. This platter with a lively pattern is not in the English style. It is indistinctly signed, possibly 'Loes', and may be a Swiss creation.

Ox-eye. This carver developed a unique style, characterised by the elements being small-scale, with lively tendrils and twisting poppy leaves. It shows a revival of naturalism with less ear and more stalk, even including the nodes. There is a sister board in the collection with a different array of flora. We would love to identify the carver.

Ox-eye, circa 1930-1970, sycamore, 12 inches.

A Selection of Harvest Knives. Matching sets were certainly popular, as were ones with similar motifs.

1. A boxed ivory-handled knife, one large wheat ear on either side, the blade stamped Adams and Son, Haymarket, the box matching the blade stamp, VR, late Victorian.

2. A basic table-knife-handle shape, carved with wheat and oats to denote bread use, but not a normal handle for a bread knife. The blade is stamped 'Bread Knife, Wilcox Edgware Rd', 1850-66, bone.

3. A busy handle of wheat, rye, flowers and poppy, sold wholesale, and found in several examples with varying quality. It was a much used pattern.

4. With crisp and plumply defined hops on the upper side and vine on the under, it is a Tippler's knife! The lush carving shows no symmetry, being very naturalistic, almost in the style of Grinling Gibbons. The handle was particular to Moore, though he was not the maker. The blade is stamped: 'London made', an early feature circa 1860, and, 'James Moore, 349 Oxford St', confirms the knife as 1840-1905, with a beautiful fit of blade and handle.

5. Elegant wheat ear, berries and foliage, embedded in sweeping lines denoting leaf veins.

A selection of Harvest knives

6. The crisp, simple carving of wheat on both sides makes this handle a pleasure to hold. The blade is stamped 'Mappin Bros', making it pre-1905 when Webb joined the firm, and pre-1901 with the stamp: 'Cutlers to her Majesty'. The blade width is a luxury and, together with the handle, outshines the competition.

7. A netsuke-like handle possibly inspired by the simpler aesthetic of Japonisme, mirroring a changing taste. The handle is still in the bread knife style, but it represents a refreshing new take, with the introduction of an animal not usually depicted in fine art. It is adorned with a field mouse (see detail below right), gripping onto a ripe wheat ear, its tail looped round the stalk. A work of art, and the cream that Sheffield had to offer. The blade is stamped, Mappin Bros, and the silver ferrule with grapes is dated 1898.

8. Stamped out silver wheatsheaf handle, this hollow silver pattern was produced in vast quantities, filled with resin or a putty-like mixture, which melted with heat. Isobel gave me a lesson in washing up our Mappin table cutlery, transmitting her father's particular instructions to her as a child growing up in Glasgow in the 1950s. She had to hold the knife blade-downwards, covering the join with her finger and thumb. She had to use only warm water, and keep the blade away from sitting or running water, making a careful downward-sweeping action only, to prevent the water splashing uphill into the join. All of these precautions avoided causing the resin to melt and the blade to become detached. Birmingham 1903.

9. Highly decorated, with high-relief flowers over low-relief wheat, it is showing

A selection of harvest knives.

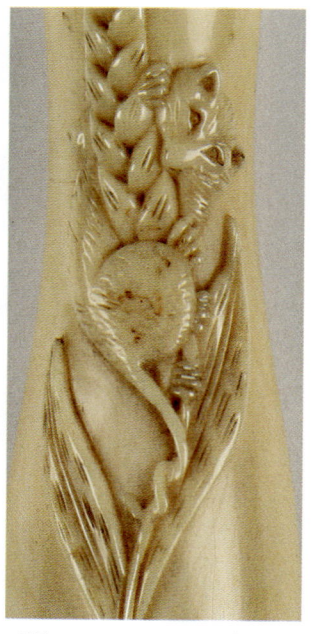

Harvest mouse (detail).

off the best of the ivory cutter's skill, including ivy and foliage for good measure. Carved all round, it is in mint condition, with the original tin finish preserved. The hefty, ivory handle was dictated by the size of the tooth.

10. With delicate wheat all round, the leaves turning back on themselves, this is an early feature on more skilful boards. The blade is stamped 'Lowcock, 38 Cornhill', dating it to 1839-1850, and is well joined.

iii) Flowers and Fruit

Strawberry blossom, with foliage, symmetrical, circa 1880, sycamore, 13 inches.

Lemon and herbaceous border, an unusual combination, circa 1880, sycamore, 11 ½ inches.

Apples and pears, deeply carved and twiggy, circa 1880, sycamore, 12 inches.

3 wheat 3 flowers, in triangular formation, with a lot of movement circa 1880, sycamore, 12 inches.

A selection of floral knives.

1. A butter knife, the handle with an extremely delicate rendition of an iris-like flower.

2. A bluebell knife, a rare woodland flower to find on a handle, boxwood.

3. A spray of poppies in boxwood, a lighter handle, better for a smaller hand-grip.

4. A bell-shaped flower, possibly another bluebell and wheat. Sycamore handle, used for cheaper items as it is not as hard as box wood, but the carving is very fine.

5. A handle with bell-shaped flowers on one side and wheat on the back, boxwood, the handle fitting perfectly with the blade, without a ferrule, clearly conceived to go together. The blade is stamped: Benham of Wigmore St.

6. A very fine knife with an ivory handle of a lively daffodil and wheat, surprisingly late, made in the Belle Époque, before the First World War. The ferrule is stamped: Sheffield 1914, W.Y, William Yates maker.

iv) Woodland

Oak and Mulberry. Oak is quite rare, especially when combined with what Debora Hodgson and the librarians at RHS Wisley kindly suggested was *Morus nigra*, the black mulberry, although the leaves are rather narrow.

Oak and mulberry. circa 1870, sycamore, 12 ½ inches.

Holly and wheat. A rare holly board (only two are known). Wing's catalogue has one, circa 1880, sycamore, 13 inches.

Hazelnuts and fruits of the wood, with a banner that is too worn to read, circa 1880, sycamore, 13 inches.

Ivy leaves all round, asymmetrical and naturalistic, with an attractively turned back, sycamore, 13 inches.

A crumb brush, attesting to the fashion for all things wooden. It is designed as an oak branch, delicately curved and carved with undulating leaves, the naturalistic handle formed of the twig looping around, 13 ½ inches.

A Selection of Woodland Knives. It goes without saying, a woodland board absolutely must be accompanied by a woodland knife.
1. Ivy twines around both sides with clusters of berries and spirally tendrils. Delicate and asymmetrical, the background looks like bark, 'A&N VR Bread Knife'.

2. A very fine handle decorated on all sides with lily of the valley, demonstrating unstinting quality. By Mappin and Webb, one of the most prestigious cutlers. They would have had their own handles made uniquely for them and made to fit the blade.

3. A rare owl handle, associated with keeping the field mice down, like a scarecrow, the handle becoming the trunk, with wheat on both flanks.

4. An ivory handle with ivy and fruit all round, similar to the wooden version, the silver ferrule is stamped JB.

5. Fern fronds on a spiral. Ferns were very popular as house plants in the mid-1800s, a craze which led to over-collection and it had to be forbidden. Boxwood, Joseph Rodgers & Sons, Sheffield.

5.

ORIGINS

Mesolithic to Georgian Tableware

The Elusive First Board. No amount of digging in the museums and archives of Europe and the States revealed texts or visuals pinpointing 'the first breadboard ever made'. Either it was never recorded, or it is out there still awaiting discovery, and we hope this book might widen the list of interested parties who are game to share their discoveries. While hunting, Rosslyn collected information on the precursors of breadboards, and came to the conclusion that they were a very English fusion of multipurpose chopping boards, showy serving platters and individual trencher plates.

From Mesolithic Times. Our ancestors made do with multipurpose chopping boards made of stumps and lumps of tree. Any handy bit of wood would have served, in the same way that during the Medieval period – according to the English historian, Dr Lucy Worsley – people used the same room for everything. A traditional alternative which dispensed with the knife, was to pull the bread apart, called 'breaking bread'. We associate this now with baguettes and Judeo-Christian rituals. Yet another variation, which bypassed the need for a board, consisted of holding the loaf up close and sawing inwards. This method was reportedly still used by some grannies in the 1960s, from Sheffield in England to rural Westphalia in Germany. Kitchen tables also served for cutting bread in France.

Plate by George Lailey, Berkshire, elm, 1930s, considerable warping, 10 inches.

Bodging. In families where a board was considered necessary for the sharing of bread, bodgers provided a cheap solution. This tradition – of working the forests and making practical wooden implements for everyday use – is carried on by skilled craftspeople such as Robin Wood, but is on the Heritage Crafts Endangered List. One such 'bodger', named George Lailey (1869–1958), made his livelihood from this woodcraft and became a local celebrity in and around Bucklebury Common, in Berkshire. Active during the early 1900s, he produced tableware from locally-hewn elm, using a pole lathe. Lailey used the same tools and methods as were current centuries ago, making his creations ageless (and undateable to the uninitiated). A charming example of his work was kindly donated to our museum by Martin Fletcher, a forester. Made in the 1930s, this small plate with a shallow lip was turned simply and is a good example of what chopping boards, platters and plates probably looked like for thousands of years. Mr Fletcher's mother bought it from the Bucklebury bowl-man's workshop, a wooden hut at Turners Green, Upper Bucklebury, and she used it as her breadboard for most of her married life. Lailey's tools and lathe are now on view at the Museum of Rural Life, Reading.

1: Roman table treen

Fragments of round wooden plates (*legno tornito*) miraculously survived the eruption at Pompeii. They were photographed by Rosslyn at the Museo Archeologico Nazionale di Napoli during a privileged back stage visit. Their parallel concentric grooves turned on a lathe served as delicate ornamentation, and are very similar to the simple embellishments on this 18th century platter, illustrating how little styles changed over 1,700 years. Rosslyn returned from Naples fizzing with excitement, recounting how she had also been shown the carbonised bread and had touched it with her bare hands before the Curator plied her with gloves!

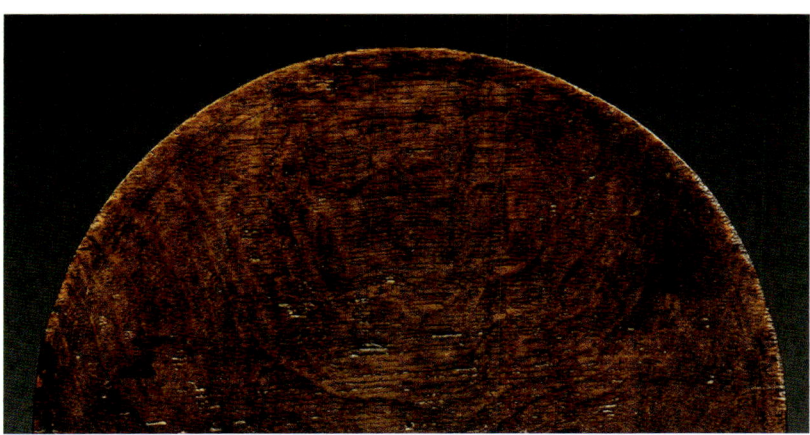

Platter (detail), 18th century, oak, 12 inches.

2: Germanic buns and plates

The Anglo-Saxon tribes ate simply and in the 1000s, we see a selection of shapes on the feast table of Abraham in the *Old English Illustrated Hexateuch* (BM:022580). Small circles and a semi-circle suggest buns. There are rectangular items among the large round serving dishes which may be individual trenchers of wood for placing choice cuts from the roast or sharing pot.

Later on in the century, their cousins, the Normans, immortalised themselves feasting smugly on English soil while Harold hurried back down from the North. Bishop Odo is blessing the large sacred loaf on the left of William, while individuals again ate buns of manchet bread. Darker brown rectangular and square objects placed randomly on the table may represent plates as above.

Detail of the Bayeux Tapestry. By special authorisation of the Ville de Bayeux.

3: Medieval trenchers made of bread

By 1508 in the *Boke of Keruynge*, a great ritual was being recorded around the art of cutting stale brown bread into single-use plates for the nobility to eat their meaty morsels off. Once sodden with juices, the 'pantler' (bread butler) would gather them all up and hand them to the poor, thronging at the kitchen door. The trenchers were rectangular and appear in illustrations of feasts and in manuals of table customs.

It is not clear if the first individual plates of the Normans and Saxons were also of sliced stale bread, or of wood. It is conjecture, but possibly the two were used concurrently, to distinguish the rich from the poor. Trenchers of bread might have indicated top-ranking individuals by their conspicuous consumption. It can be confirmed that the poor boys of Winchester College used wood in 1416, according to the purchase record, which lists 10 dozen 'Disci lignei', or rounds of wood, the first ever mention of them, costing 2s 7d.

Solomon's Feast, 1491 (detail), with the pantler offering sliced bread-plates with a *presentoire* knife, rounded at the tip to avoid accident or assassination. Metropolitan Museum of Art, New York.

4: Tudor trenchers of wood for the main course

The wastefulness must have become unsustainable because by the 1500s the nobility had returned to wood. Not only that, a number of ground-breaking innovations were in evidence: individual plates were larger, to carry the whole meal at once rather than mouthful by mouthful. A large – if shallow – round depression was gouged out to retain sauce and stop the peas going to the dogs. The Renaissance really did free the mind, right down to solving personal conundrums of this sort.

Queen Elizabeth had the grandest one of all, of course, which is described and illustrated as follows: 'The great round standeth upon 4 small pillars almost 2 inches hye off the square. The lesser round standeth above the square an inch and a quarter and it is made in fashion of a bell with the great end upward.'

Anybody who was anybody had dozens of them. All tableware was sold in sets of twelve, mimicking the Last Supper, which is why thirteen is unlucky. The wealthy were also allowed the luxury of an additional small depression for their personal supply of salt. Abingdon's Aldermen ordered a bulk consignment for their yearly banquet in 1556. Square trenchers remained in use into the early 1800s. The scholars of Winchester College still use them, according to our guest Hilary.

Wooden trencher, 'It feels like beech', late 1600s, 10 ¾ inches.

Dessert roundel, possibly a reproduction from the early 1800s, 1 of 6, mixed woods, 7 inches.

5: Tudor trenchers of wood for dessert

The Tudors were positively on fire: next they brought in little decorative wooden roundels for sugared delicacies. Sugar was the latest craze for the wealthy few, and special 'Banqueting Halls' were built just for the dessert course, with windows placed high off the ground to prevent servants witnessing the sugar-fuelled romps! A new plate for a new course meant no more mopping up or flipping over. The real break with tradition was making them decorative, with one side left plain for food, the other painted with flowers, fruits, foliage and verses. All to glorify sugar. Thus begins the diversification of plates in earnest. This part-set (above right) is not Elizabethan, but is possibly a Regency recreation, made during the Tudor Revival as a prop for Tudor feasts, or later.

6: Georgian coasters and dessert dishes

With the arrival of porcelain, the Georgians mostly relegated wood to the everyday. But there were certain wooden items which never got retired such as coasters with little brass castors for wheeling heavy items up and down the table, possibly whole Stiltons or large flagons.

There might have been a retro-trend for turned and beautifully carved wooden tableware, which provided the inspiration for bread-platters later on. This daintily-carved dessert dish (below left) would have been used for fruit, dried fruit and sweets. The carving is masterly, with steady concentric lines to indicate basket weave, a tad uneven to feel natural, but not too much to seem amateur. A virtuoso balancing act!

The tankard in the shape of a stook of wheat (below right), made up of many bundles, was a marketing gimmick of the Wheatsheaf Inn in the Midlands.

Left: Dessert dish, private collection, mahogany, 6 1/4 inches. Right: Beer tankard, 1761, Owen Evan-Thomas Collection (courtesy Stobart Davies).

7: Georgian plates and salvers

This period saw a mouth-watering influx of new flavours and foods as the world opened up. With the new wealth came a need to store and present precious ingredients such as tea, chocolate, coffee and spices. Wooden plates, often of sycamore or beech, continued in use for informal purposes. The shallow circular depression from Tudor times evolved over 200 years into a deep lip for catching most things. The robust round trencher board (see below) was a sort of multipurpose kitchen board that predates breadboards. It was likely used for both chopping on and eating off, with saw marks on both sides.

While wooden plates were still plain, silversmiths were making bread salvers. Inventories of the British Embassies to Prussia and Paris in the early 1820s mention bread salvers among the silver plate. It would not be long before the skilled woodcarvers of the age would be combining the delicacy of such silverwork with the robustness and lightness of wood.

So after 2,000 years of being content with relatively plain wooden plates, dishes and platters, what was it that sparked a need for something ornate, exclusively for bread? It is possible bread-platters were an artistic response to the political and economic crises spanning the 1740s-1840s in France and Britain.

Round trencher board, sycamore, late 18th century, 11 inches.

Victorian Politics and the Corn Laws

1: The Corn Laws

Famine. Fluctuating grain prices had been causing misery throughout the 1700s due to numerous bad harvests, eventually sparking revolution in France, which was as much about cheap bread as *Liberté, Egalité, Fraternité*. The Napoleonic Wars exacerbated things with trade blockades from 1803, lasting twelve years, until the Allies of Europe defeated Napoleon at Waterloo. In an attempt to replenish the coffers, and in a spasm of patriotism, Parliament, which consisted of the great landowners, passed the 'Corn Laws'. These protectionist trade tariffs raised the price of foreign wheat entering the UK, creating a local monopoly for British producers.

Rapacious Rich. Rather than keep the prices manageable, they raised them such that only the richest could afford bread, making it a prized commodity and status symbol. Bread had been a staple for breakfast since the 1720s, and tea since the 1780s, across all social strata, so the poor felt the deprivation bitterly. For thirty-one years they turned to potato, barley, rye and oats. But more poor harvests and the Enclosure Acts meant both the urban and rural poor were becoming destitute. The Peterloo demonstration was crushed mercilessly and protesters hanged. Lord Melbourne refused to budge on the Laws 'unless strongly demanded by public opinion'.

The Invention Theory. Within this dire back-drop, an unattractive trait of human nature must be mentioned: the irresistible desire to show off. More specifically, let us consider the habit of commissioning artists to make objets d'art to store and present our most precious possessions. So for example, keeping to the realms of wood and food, much time and money has been spent through the centuries on carving beautiful receptacles and gadgets for salt, spices, sugar, nuts, chocolate, tea and coffee. If we follow the logic, then it is easy to imagine that the super-rich of 1820s Britain would have felt a natural urge to buy something showy to present their precious loaves. And 'present' is the key word, as 'bread-platters' had depressions in the centre, with raised, carved edges, which suggests carvers expected the users to simply present their buns and pre-cut slices.

Opportunism. Carvers were entrepreneurs who would have had their finger on the pulse, and been constantly on the lookout for new lines and design innovations. We think they survived the bread famine by thinking up such new concepts as beautiful platters, exclusively for presenting bread. Happily, the trend caught on among the rich who saw them as must-have status symbols.

The Invention of a New Bread-Cutting Ritual. The collection contains examples of such platters with the carving badly worn by knife marks. We propose, and are quite prepared to be shot down, that the back-office work of pre-cutting bread may have been promoted to the dining table or side board, to add extra flourish to the bread-sharing moment. This novelty would have been part of the penchant for specialised tableware, driven itself by the Victorian trend for specialised rooms for every aspect of life, containing all the appropriate homewares and embellishments.

2: The Repeal of the Corn Laws

Richard Cobden. Enter Mr Richard Cobden (1804-65), a Sussex farmer's son who became a leading figure in British politics. Cobden called these unpopular laws 'legislative murder', and founded the Anti-Corn Law League in 1838 with nine others, including the Radical and Liberal politician John Bright. As the League's leading figurehead, Cobden described his opponents as 'the landlords, the bread-taxing oligarchy, unprincipled, unfeeling, rapacious and plundering'. His opponents described the League as a 'cunning, unscrupulous, knavish, pestilent body of men'.

Richard Cobden MP.

The Anti-Corn Law League. The League toured the country raising awareness with public talks, trying to galvanise the starving public into action to get the Corn Laws repealed. Cobden reported to Parliament on the inhumane consequences of the Laws, giving detailed accounts about unaffordable weekly expenses. He championed free trade, not only to save the poor from starving, but as a way of avoiding future wars. According to his theory, if a country saw a glut of something in a neighbouring country, the only way to acquire the commodity was to fight it out, unless there was a trade relationship allowing them to purchase it legitimately and peacefully.

Rallying Artists. In a *Punch* cartoon, *The Premiere's Fix* of 1845, the prime minister Robert Peel is to be found cowering high on a fence: on one side 'Agriculture' is championed by a raging bull bearing the face of the Duke of Richmond, while on the other 'Free Trade' is embodied by two snarling dogs with 'Cobden' and 'Bright' around their collars.

By coincidence the collection contains a finely carved bread knife, its much-worn handle in the shape of a dog standing on its rear legs, clutching a large ear of wheat. The College of Arms confirmed it is not one of their emblems. Cobden is often depicted in *Punch* cartoons with a sprig of wheat about his person, the symbol of his new League. Could the bread knife be a piece of political activism?

John Henry Verinder, the cutler, was active from the early 1820s, at 79 St Paul's

'The Premier's Fix', *Punch*, 1845.
Punch Cartoon Library/TopFoto.

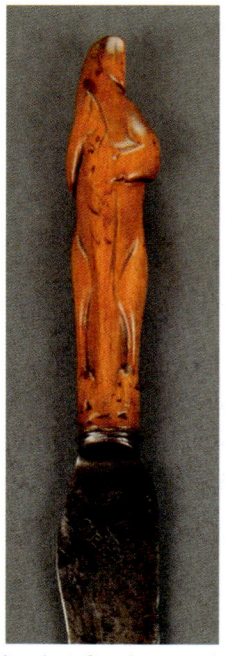

Verinder knife, dog and wheat
handle, c1840s, boxwood.

Churchyard and later in Ludgate Hill. He was honoured with the title of Master Cutler from 1828 and 'Company's Cutler' in 1835 and 1846, supplying all the cutlery to the Cutler's Company for their dinners at the Hall. A powerful man, then, possibly using his art to drum up support for Cobden's campaign.

To Wheat or Not to Wheat. A snippet in *The Art-Union* magazine of 1848 describes how bread-platters can be 'bordered only with groups of corn differently arranged. Many have been executed by the order of noblemen and gentlemen, when family mottos and crests have been substituted'. It is extraordinary to imagine the broiling atmosphere of the 1840s when choosing or avoiding a wheat design for one's breadboard was super-charged with class identity and political allegiance.

Blight and Repeal. After nine years of campaigning, the Peel government was brought down, the Corn Laws repealed and there was suddenly a surfeit of wheat available at affordable prices. The decision was certainly precipitated by the final nail in the coffin: potato blight. It spread across the UK in 1845-6, causing mass starvation in Ireland, just when potato had come to replace bread among the poor. There were horrific stories of dogs scavenging amongst the graves.

Richmond Protests. The tariff was reduced from 40 shillings to 10s to 4s, before being removed completely. The Duke of Richmond took the news very ill and vented in Parliament in May 1846 that the Lords should appeal to the country: '…to turn out of Parliament every one of the ninety-seven deserters – in fact, the whole of the 110 who followed Sir Robert Peel – men, who, if they had been in the army in India, would have abandoned their colours, as they had here run away from their principles'. Rip-off Britain was quashed, for the time being.

Richmond's Bread-Platter. Despite all the Monopolist gloom about the demise of agriculture, the Duke (see Cobden's Bees-wing, Richmond's Black-draught, Punch, 1846) was clearly flush enough in 1848 to buy himself a top-of-the-range bread-platter from Mr William Gibbs Rogers, costing at least a guinea, customised with the word 'Glenfiddich'. This was pre-distillery days, so no reference to his preferred tipple was intended. Clearly his favourite part of the Gordon-Lennox estate, he would organise hunting parties at Glenfiddich Lodge and possibly his bread-platter was part of the kit he kept there, or at the Castle to remind him of it. If you have their bread-platter, do get in touch!

Peace and Plenty. *Punch*'s cartoon of 1850, 'The Free-Trader's Valentine' contains a poem with the phrase 'Peace and Plenty'. This pithy motto is simple yet a profound celebration of what humanity needs to flourish, and what seems out of our grasp so often through history. The board may have been carved as a defiant 'Hurrah!' to the end of the Napoleonic Wars and the Corn Laws. It also resonates with Psalms 147:14 'He grants peace to your borders and satisfies you with the finest wheat'. The agricultural elite had feared its own pauperisation, but in an interview with a farmer, the tone was more optimistic: 'We shall turn our land and our brains to better account', ending their torpor under the Reign of Protection. Their complacency counted against the landed classes eventually as they were, many of them, unable to adapt to a more enterprise-driven society. The Duke of Richmond's family was reduced to selling their family seat, Gordon Castle, along with the contents in the 1930s.

'Peace and Plenty', sycamore, circa 1800s, 11 ¾ inches.

'In Memory of Richard Cobden', circa 1865, the year of his death, sycamore 12 ½ inches.

Cobden's Legacy. Richard Cobden brought plenty to the country, but he bankrupted himself in the process. Again the British people rallied behind their hero and a collection was made enabling him to buy back his childhood home. Tellingly, Victoria never gave him a pension, although she offered him a Baronetcy – which he declined. His only London statue is in Camden Town. But Cobden graciously said on Peel's resignation: 'If the RH Baronet [Peel] chooses to retire from office in consequence of this vote, he carries with him the esteem and gratitude of a larger number of the population of this Empire than ever followed any Minister that was ever hurled from power. This is one of the most magnificent reforms carried out in any country.' *Punch's* cartoon, 'Monument to Peel' in 1850, to mark his death, consists of a vast stack of loaves and the words 'Cheap Bread', with Cobden looking on as the facilitator.

'**In Memory of Richard Cobden**'. There couldn't be a more perfect place to commemorate Cobden's victory than on a breadboard. The lettering is unusual in that it is all capitals and resembles the Roman serifs of a tombstone. It may have been made in 1865, the year of his death, or an anniversary thereof. A visitor suggested a middle class townsman may have carved it, grateful for the new lease of life given to him and his workers. The letters are spaced irregularly, the words are too far apart and the lines are furry, suggesting an amateur. Clearly, breadboards were still politically charged twenty years after the Repeal of the Corn Laws! Coincidentally, it was in the 1860s that breadboards really took off, because the populace finally had bread, and the new generation of carvers made them into a cheap, cheerful, practical way to celebrate cocking a snook at the Establishment.

Righting a Wrong. The victory of poor over rich, right over might, was still reverberating 50 years on, and rightly remains a part of our GCSE History curriculum. Visitors may have forgotten names and dates, but I only have to say 'The Repeal of the…' for one guest to always pipe up triumphantly '…Corn Laws!' Probably the only Repeal worth knowing in over 1,500 years of law-making. On 1 August 1896, the village of Denby Dale made a 'Jubilee Pie' to commemorate the 50th anniversary of the repeal of the Corn Laws. The pie was ten feet long, six and a half feet wide, and a foot deep.

Denby Dale Pie souvenir plate, 1896, 10 inches.

157

6.

ARTISTS IN WOOD

William Gibbs Rogers (1792-1875)

The Victorian Grinling Gibbons

William Gibbs Rogers (WGR) had a stellar career carving commissions for royalty and aristocracy around Europe, from a cradle for Queen Victoria's latest child, to embellishments for the Turkish Sultan's new Palace in Istanbul. He refurbished whole churches, restored rotting Grinling Gibbons carvings across the country, was a Fine Arts Annotator for the Great Exhibition of 1951 and was rewarded with a pension from the Queen.

He made a name for himself miniaturising the magic of Gibbons and applied it to dozens of household items such as a frames, spoons, potato bowls, furniture, panelling and brackets. Anyone with a guinea to spare could acquire a portable, useful chunk of Gibbons-like profusion. Gibbons' focus on the

William Gibbs Rogers holding conch shells (a favourite subject of Grinling Gibbons) 1832. It is possible WGR carved the frame. Private collection by descent.

natural world stemmed from the Puritan rejection of religious imagery in the 1660s. With the increasingly wealthy urban middle classes wishing to 'keep up with the Jones's', but without the vast houses, WGR was assured a healthy stream of commissions.

Surprisingly, he – or his workshop – also produced bread-platters, 'in considerable quantities' through the 1840s, although he claims to have been making them 'on a less extensive scale…for many years', so, say, from the late 1820s. It is as early as Rosslyn's evidence goes, so we would love to hear from you if you have information on bread-platters predating this. In total, eighteen different WGR bread-platter designs are described across all the source materials Rosslyn found, and they are covered in this section.

Early years: 1807-1847

Ship to Shore. Creative and practical, WGR was apprenticed to a shipwright in London. The industry was booming in 1807, as the Napoleonic Wars raged and Napoleon's plan for a Channel Tunnel was somewhat less palatable! However he found himself drawn to the decorative side of woodcarving, visiting many London churches and St Paul's Cathedral to admire the 'light, bold' swags of Gibbons. A few early contracts for royalty and nobility set him off with a thriving workshop in Soho in 1817.

WGR's Wood Revival. He appeared at a time when, according to *The Art-Union*, the country's only fine art magazine, woodcarving was a 'long-neglected branch of ornamental art', and he was later credited not only with reviving it, but also personifying it. Prince Albert, a tireless patron of the arts, also promoted woodcarving. At his suggestion, 'prizes were offered for…works of artisans, not professional wood carvers…with a view to encouraging home occupation, such as prevail in Switzerland and Germany, secondary to other pursuits'.

Woodcarving for Westminster. The immense job of embellishing Barry's new Parliament interiors went out to tender in 1844 and WGR submitted proposals. Although he was not selected, the judges did concede he would have been the best man for the job. He lost the contract to Pugin, who was not a carver, and who died in 1852 from overwork, after a brief stay in Bedlam. Barry's Neo-Gothic palace set the tone for much of the century, and certainly affected WGR's known bread-platters, all of which were lettered in the Gothic style. Despite losing that job, he landed the refurbishment of St Michael's Cornhill, in the City of London, and posed for a souvenir photo with his eagle lectern, which was later exhibited in the Great Exhibition of 1851.

WGR with his eagle lectern for St Michael's Cornhill, exhibited at the 1851 Great Exhibition, from his portfolio.

Charitable Activities. Woodcarvers had no Guild or Worshipful Company to shield them from adversity. Thus WGR used his position as an influencer to become a trustee of the Virtuosi Provident Fund, and a supporter of the Institute of Fine Arts and the London Institution. For a soirée at the latter, he brought along some 'contributions to the library table' in the form of some 'carved bread-trenchers'. They must have engendered lively conversation, just as our museum does today! He was probably also active in the Woodcarvers Society, set up in his neighbourhood in 1833, which aimed to educate and care for his fraternity. Henry Mayhew visited the Society during his research on *London Labour and the London Poor* and found it 'a place of beauty, refinement, comfort, intelligence and ease'. WGR lived and breathed his art, so much so that his home became a museum and open-house, bursting with sculptures and carvings, for entertaining clients and educating carvers who had no access to books or art.

WGR's Church Accessories. Prince Albert's Christian Revival meant churches were benefitting from increased footfall and began major restoration and investment projects. WGR received many commissions for alms platters and altar plates for presenting the Communion bread; his bread-and-butter between larger commissions no doubt. The dish is worth illustrating here as its style of carving gives us valuable insights into what his bread-platters could have looked like. For example, the Gothic lettering with curlicues is reminiscent of other pieces connected with his workshop. *The Art-Union*, quoting WGR, notes that: 'alms dishes of this mode of fabrication are becoming favourites, and that numerous churches, particularly in the neighbourhood of Oxford, have been supplied with them from this atelier'. Regarding another alms dish appearing in one of his house sale catalogues, *The Art-Union* remarks that: 'as ecclesiastical appurtenances, the alms-dishes, sacramental plates and alms-boxes of Gothic character, must be noticed of correct design and careful execution'.

Alms dish by WGR, carved wood, *The Art-Union*, December 1847.

The Middleton Bread-platter: 1848

WGR's Bread-Platters. *The Art-Union* keeps us on tenterhooks when admiring some of his bread-platters: 'We rejoice to find the most accomplished wood-carver of the age directing his attention to matters comparatively trivial, but still of great importance as a means of education to pure taste in Art. The fame of Mr. W.G. Rogers has been established by works of a far higher order; but these objects of daily use have all the qualities of grace of design and delicacy of finish, which distinguish his more elaborate performances.' Despite the dearth of contemporary visuals, we

163

are very pleased to have located two precious examples of his bread-platters, with sure provenance; one in the collection and the other in NSW, Australia.

WGR and the Middleton Platter, 1848. The 'Middleton platter' is the oldest dateable board in the collection and one of the earliest pieces to earn wall space in Rosslyn's crowded home. It was one of many 'executed by the order of noblemen and gentlemen' and is referred to in *The Art-Union* as follows: 'We may mention a number [of boards] which have been produced for special positions…a second for the Countess of Jersey [Sarah Sophia Child] with the name Middleton.' Middleton referred to the Countess's country seat of Middleton Park in Oxfordshire. (See 'Status Symbols' in the 'Mottos and Motifs' section.)

The two Earl's coronets, defining her and her husband's rank, are delicate and sensuous with distinct lines. The Gothic lettering of 'Middleton' is eccentric,

The Middleton Platter, by WGR, limewood, 1848, 13 inches.

with a prolonged twiggy ascender on the 'd'. Although naturally light-coloured, this board has been darkened, possibly with walnut stain, which WGR's son recommends specifically for limewood in his book, *The Art of Woodcarving: Practical Hints to Amateurs and a Short History of the Art* (1867): 'Walnut stain (made without oil) is in very general use for lime and other light woods; it can be diluted with water to any tint required, and should be put on the carving with a brush or small camel-hair pencil'.

Limewood and Bread Rituals. WGR most likely chose this soft, crisp-carving wood because he had some left over from a restoration job on some Grinling Gibbons pendants. As George Rogers put it in his book on woodcarving: 'Lime wood was almost exclusively used by Grinling Gibbons for all his magnificent drops and festoons of fruit, flowers, and birds at Petworth, Chatsworth, Burghley, Belton, Melbury, Gatton, and the numerous other noble seats to which his genius has imparted such a charm.' The wood's softness and the board's raised decorative border both imply that he was not expecting his client to cut bread on it. The platter may have been used at first by a footman like a tray, for presenting buns, rolls or pre-cut slices to guests. The slicing was probably happening at the sideboard on a plain board on request, and the slices were then transferred. There may have been a transition phase wherein patrons began bypassing the plain board and cutting directly on the decorative one, but the carvers were still producing platters in softer woods. This might explain why the Middleton platter, ill-adapted though it is, shows much scoring.

WGR and his Sons

1. Frederick, 1855

'The FMR board' is equally exceptional in that it has a watertight provenance; it is an heirloom handed down from Rogers' son, Frederick Horace Rogers (the 'F R'), and is still in the possession of his descendants. He emigrated to Australia at the tender age of nineteen and married Mary Minton Long (the 'M') in Hobart Town on 18 May 1855. The family is unclear why he left at such a young age. Nevertheless, the family could not miss the opportunity of presenting him with his own customised wedding board. Joyce Stephenson has spent many years reuniting the descendents of William Gibbs Rogers and collating research. She put Rosslyn in touch with his family, residing in Brooman via Milton, NSW, who still own the board and kindly took this photograph of it propped up against the barby. The 'M' bears a great similarity with the 'M' in Middleton, both resembling a bishop's mitre. Signature lettering was a subtle way for carvers to identify their creations.

'FMR' wedding board, 1855, private collection, NSW, Australia

Simple and Effective. The board has a lush wheat theme, with a simple reduced pattern. It is a cheaper model, experimenting with new ideas such as fewer motifs, to throw the existing shapes into definition. A carver's challenge is how to fill the border without ending up either with excess or a mean look. Certainly the Victorian style followed the tenet: 'Nature abhors a vacuum', which often led to decorative overload.

New Look. Clients' complaints about wear and tear from cutting on their bread-platters would have eventually prompted carvers to adapt the design. Note the raised central cutting area, mostly worn away, the sloping border and the choice of sycamore. This breadboard heralded the 'New Look' for what became the quintessential British breadboard. By 1871, WGR's son even mentions in his woodcarving book: ' Sycamore…is greatly, and, in fact, principally used for bread plates and potato bowls and other articles, when a light tint is a consideration.'

Bread-Platters vs Bread Boards vs Bread Plates vs Breadboards. There is a confusion about the terms which might be worth clearing up. The Victorians used the term 'bread-platter' to refer to elegant salvers of wood, ceramic, silver or glass for serving communal bread, with a central depression and a raised border. The Victorian understanding of 'bread board' was a long baker's plank for delivering loaves, which was hoisted on a shoulder and proved useful for darting along crowded pavements.

The additional term, 'bread plate', used above by G.A. Roberts in 1871, suggests a more compact breadboard or dish had also appeared which could slot in the plate rack. In the 1930s the words 'bread board' had evolved to mean a more practical bread-platter where the cutting surface was raised and the border sloped away to preserve the carving. The two terms were interchangeable for a while, before 'platter' was dropped. The author is proud to announce the launch of a whole new closed compound noun, 'breadboard', to honour the upcoming bicentenary of this understated but much cherished piece of British food culture. If we all use the word enough, it will get in the OED!

2. William Harry (1825-73)

William Harry Rogers 'WHR' is referred to as WGR's 'Designer', before branching out into book design. WGR 'has latterly turned his attention to the Italian style, and, assisted by his eldest son, Harry Rogers, who is well known as a prolific and good designer, has produced some important works'. We have identified similarities between the designs of WHR, many of which were illustrated in *The Art-Union*, and some finely-carved items in the collection.

Bulrush butterdish.

Bulrush pew end.
Courtesy of Joyce A. Stephenson.

Bulrushes Butter Dish and Pew End. The presence of bulrushes on a number of his household wares echoes the treatment of the same flora on this butter dish. The bulrush leaves double back on themselves across all the items – a skilful feat to pull off convincingly in carving. The popularity of his designs for the oak interior of St Michael's Church, Cornhill, London, possibly inspired WGR's carvers to create tableware with similar motifs as a sideline. The pew ends were especially original, with fruits and flowers carved from nature alongside religious themes.

3. George Alfred (1837-97)

George Alfred, WGR's youngest son, followed him into the carving business and became highly esteemed in his turn. *The Art-Union* continued its patronage of the family, giving us a visual record of his achievements. We have no direct references to GAR bread-platters, but when WGR retired in 1865, it is assumed his son continued carving them, especially since they became a national craze from the 1860s.

Convolvulus frame and bread-platter. He produced and signed an exquisite convolvulus frame, when bindweed was a popular symbol of love and friendship.

Totally in the style of Gibbons, for its naturalism and lack of symmetry, the exquisite 3-D fretted carving makes the convolvulus come alive. The breadboard (page 168) is of a similar quality, stamped A. Barrett & Sons, 63-64 Piccadilly. Barrett is listed at this address by 1865 as a brush and comb manufacturer, importer of sponges and travel equipment. It could easily have been made by GAR for this retailer. Close examination of both items reveals that the convolvulus flowers are almost identical to those appearing on the Bulrush Butterdish featured above. The convolvulus leaves are even veined in surprisingly similar ways.

Wheat and Poppies Frame and Bread-Platter. GAR, 'who has succeeded his venerable father' in the business, exhibited a poppy and wheat frame at the Paris Universal Exhibition of 1872. The illustration made it into *The Art-Union* and the exhibition catalogue. The collection has a board displaying a similar combination of motifs, possibly copied from pattern books of the time. The striking feature of the frame is that the poppy heads are bold and exaggerated in size and the wheat small, to create perspective. Likewise the bread-platter (below) is an explosion of fertility and joy for a good harvest, in one swishing design, with no lines of symmetry, where every poppy is different, and every ear of wheat is unique. It is very deeply carved, possibly of limewood. The significance of the

poppy was twofold: firstly it was a joyous sign of a good harvest, and secondly it was tolerated despite being a weed, because farmers used the poppy seeds to add to the bread, making sure nothing went to waste.

The Art of Woodcarving. GAR published a book on the subject to encourage amateurs to get carving and was also teaching 'Ladies' and 'Gentlemen', not just his apprentices. He just hints at the subtle difficulty of naturalistic carving: 'the experienced carver will translate, as it were, the [natural shape]…by his judgement without losing its characteristics, but merely arranging it in such a manner as will make it possible to render its representation in wood practicable and effective. In fact it is sometimes necessary to exaggerate forms to counterbalance the want of colour in our material'. The poppy and wheat frame appears in it as a possible idea for his fledgling readers to attempt! A review of the book in *The Lady's Own Paper* of 1867 says: 'Ladies interested in the art of carving – that of late has become quite fashionable – will do well to consult Mr Rogers' book.' Another review in *The Saturday Review* states: 'Mr G.A. Rogers…the well-known wood-carver, to whom and whose father much of the English revival of the art is owing.' More gushing yet, the *Pall Mall Gazette*: 'Mr Rogers and his family in a great degree represent the carving art of this country.' The book went into four editions. In the 1881 Census, GAR described himself as 'Master Woodcarver', with one wife and three assistants living at 29 Maddox Street, London.

WGR's Other Platters

WGR's Bread-Platters for the Nobility, 1848. Another couple of one-offs are recorded, one of which included an 'exquisite finish for the Duke of Richmond (see 'Origins' section for his role in the Corn Law debate), and which was inscribed in ornamental letters with the word 'Glenfiddich'. A third, more remarkable than the rest, was for Sir Robert Menzies, and had as a motto in Saxon characters, 'VIL GOD I ZAL' (With God's will, I shall). Sadly, neither board is to be found among the residual collections of these two great estates.

WGR's Bread-Platters for Exhibitions. The catalogue for the Great Exhibition lists one of WGR's bread-platters with the motto: 'All with one Accord in one Place', which was suggested by Mrs Rogers. It was also available in French and German and was priced at '1l.1s.' – in other words a guinea, or a pound and a shilling. For the Dublin Exposition of 1854, he offered a selection including:
'Waste Not Want Not' (10 shillings).
'Take this and be Thankful' (12s).

'Man doth not Live by Bread Alone' (12s).

'Dominus Providebit' (10s).

'Bread is the Staff of Life' in double line letters (1 guinea).

'Indian wheat platter, highly finished' (£2 10s).

To put these breadboard prices into context, it is eye-opening to find that the salary of a Victorian maid-of-all-work in the 1850s with bed and board amounted to no more than £6 per annum.

WGR's Off-the-Peg Bread-Platters

Described by *The Art-Union* as 'old friends', there were clearly certain designs which proved popular across the decades, and which are described in some detail, in a gushing article that gives us a rare list of his boards on display in New Bond Street in 1848. The collection contains a few pieces which have similar mottos or motifs and are handsomely carved to a high standard. We cannot attribute them precisely, but they are certainly 'of the School of' WGR.

1. The Staff of Life Platter

'The Staff of Life', oak, stamped J.D.M., circa 1850, 15 inches.

The Staff of Life. *The Art-Union* article mentions one such platter, 'encircled by such mottos as "Bread is the Staff of Life" [...] in raised letters of old English character'. The Staff of Life platter is special for its great size. The full moulding is noticeable for its generous width – an extravagance, given that there is not much carving-room to play with on a breadboard.

It was destined for bread, given the motto, and the lettering shows similarities with the Middleton board, especially the 't' and 'l', where they both split into serifs at the tip, with a scroll on the left. The diamond shaped bottom on the 'e' and another scroll also point towards it possibly being a Rogers' piece although the letters are broader. It would have made a bigger statement, and given the lack of cut marks, it was either used as a platter, for rolls or pre-cut items, or it was for decorative purposes only, to embellish a sideboard.

2. The Corn Platters

The Art-Union article continues: 'others are bordered only with groups of corn differently arranged'. The key is that the corn or wheat is asymmetrical, adding to its realism. The following three boards in the collection fit this description. Wheat would still have been politically charged with Corn Law symbolism in 1848, since the Repeal spear-headed by Richard Cobden was only two years past.

a) **The Wheatsheaf.** Due to extreme wear, it is difficult to be sure if it was in the early platter-style, or a board. The fact that the oak, a very hard wood, has been worn smooth to such a degree suggests it is early. Martin, our forester,

The Wheatsheaf, oak, circa 1850, worn, 12 inches.

Wheat sprigs, oak, circa 1850, worn, 12 inches.

estimated a board would lose ⅛ inch every 50 years if used daily. The surface is now a uniform flatness, but the carving would have been raised ⅛ inch higher. The scrolling acanthus is a renaissance motif. The wheat pattern is in a symmetrical half, divided vertically across the grain, with wheat in three overlapping sheaves.

b) **Wheat Sprigs.** My favourite platter. Again, there is no symmetry, with the ears appearing alone or in bunches of three, giving it a totally natural feel. Even each ear is different, as they revolve around the board all pointing in the same direction. The serving space is larger than average, with a thin border, showing generous undercutting. It has been used for cutting bread even though it compromised the carving. The wear has resulted in a superb patina.

c) **Wheat Spray.** With its very generous border, it is in the spirit and style of a Grinling Gibbons harvest pendant at Keele Hall, which WGR was commissioned to restore in the 1860s. The border leaves the cutting surface almost too small, as the lush spray of deep-carved wheat takes over, including leaves doubling

Wheat spray, circa 1860, in the style of Gibbons, sycamore, 14 inches.

back to give the feel of swaying in the breeze. While evenly spaced, every ear and stalk is differently arranged with exuberance and movement, resembling a headdress such as may have been worn by revellers at a Harvest Dinner. WGR's wheat sheaf pew end at St Michael's Cornhill is in lower relief for practicality, but is similarly a-symmetrical. Keeping the design down to one motif, gives a sense of simplicity, deceptive though it may be. It puts me very much in mind of a quotation from John Ruskin: 'As in all the arts and acts of life, the secret of high success will be found, not in a fretful and various excellence, but in a quiet singleness of justly chosen aim'.

Possible potato bowl and spoon, sycamore, 9 ¼ inches.

WGR's Potato Bowls. At first glance these are an unusual thing to get excited about, but given the recent potato famine, finding appealing ways to present potatoes at table was clearly on the agenda of those patrons of the arts who were wealthy enough to be able to afford the prized commodity. *The Art-Union* review of his pieces applauded the continued resurgence of wood for tableware and introduced these bowls as the Next Big Thing after bread-platters. 'This is certainly a novel and pleasing field for invention. We have no doubt they will become a fashionable appendage to the dinner-table'. The illustrated bowl (above) is similar to those described.

WGR's Collaborations

1. With the Potteries

Wooden Patterns. In one of WGRs' catalogues, he mentions one piece as being 'crisp enough for casting'. It is likely that these two porcelain platters were cast from Rogers originals, given the identical twiggy 'd' with the Middleton platter. They also share the same 'B'. Patterns for casting would have no undercutting, or the plaster would snag.

In answer to the question, 'Which came first, the porcelain or the wooden bread-platter?' the answer is they came together, because one required the other. It is likely that the fashion for porcelain would have led people to use porcelain plates to present their loaves, until a lighter, more robust alternative presented itself in the form of the wooden version. WGR might have used limewood to make the patterns and coated them with wax so the cast would peel away easily, and be durable enough for many uses. It's possible that supplying the potteries originally with the wooden patterns gave carvers the idea to branch out and produce examples for sale directly to retail customers. Since porcelain became popular from the 1700s onwards, bread-platters may have been in circulation well before the 1820s.

'Eat thy Bread with Joy and Thankfulness'. In the case of this motto, it is inspired from Ecclesiastes 9:7: 'Go, eat your food with gladness, and drink your

'Eat thy bread with Joy and Thankfulness', porcelain platter, 1840-90, 13 inches. | 'Give Us This Day Our Daily Bread', platter, parian, 14 x 12 ½ inches.

wine with a joyful heart, for God has already approved what you do.' But the word thankfulness has been added, probably to fill up the border.

2. With Walter Thornhill, cutler

Star Alliance. Established in 1734, Thornhill's were 'Manufacturing Cutlers' with a prestigious retail outlet at 144 New Bond Street, right near WGR at 155. WGR provided the carved components for Thornhill to assemble using his cutler's expertise. *The Art-Union* trumpets their 'accompaniment of wood and steel' as a great step forward for many fields of British manufacture. They exhibited their combos at Thornhill's gallery and at the Great Exhibition. Some of the knife handles they produced are described with 'Italian foliage executed in bas relief', and with 'Wheat alone encircled in Elizabethan ornament'. Certain superb early knives in the collection fit other descriptions, and are illustrated below, with *The Art-Union* quotations. The blades are not stamped Thornhill however. If these are indeed WGR handles, then it indicates he collaborated with other local cutlers.

A selection of early knives, fitting descriptions in *The Art-Union* of 1848.

1.'Carved wheat and poppies', boxwood, with a Georgian appearance judging by the finish of the tang. The blade is stamped 'Priest 253 Oxford Street', who was a retailer active between 1779-1915. His business was in Oxford Street from 1836-85. Size 13 ½ inches.

2. 'Wrought in the semblance of sheaves', boxwood, similar to (3), a spatula blade with a rounded end for presenting a slice of bread safely. The blade is stamped 'Kearns London', who were active at 425 Oxford Street, 1836-66. Size 14 inches.
3. 'Wrought in the semblance of sheaves', boxwood, the handle is stamped WR, which dates it to 1830-37, while the blade is stamped 'Vining 125 Regent Street London made', another upmarket retailer in the newly-built shopping mall, 1832-1850. Size 13 ½ inches.

Thornhill Sweetcorn Knife. Although not the fruit of their joint labours this knife is worthy of mention. Its handle is identical to one on a knife patented by Joseph Rodgers & Sons of Sheffield in 1848, and based on the design by the sculptor John Bell. Clearly Thornhill was buying from other cutlers, and Sheffield prices would have undercut the London makers. Compared to the original Rodgers knife (No. 1), the Thornhill knife (No. 2) has a silver ferrule, added at his request certainly. Not only does his ferrule make it more elegant, it strengthens the design at the weakest point of the handle, where most of the pressure is exerted. Bell's design pinches in at this point, making the knife even weaker. Other Joseph Rodgers & Sons knives (Nos. 3+4), in ivory and boxwood, have cracked in this very spot and been repaired. Note the considerable foreshortening of handle No. 3, due to sawing off the cracked portion before adding a strong ferrule.

A selection of sweetcorn knives, ivory and boxwood, 1848 onwards.

WGR's competitors

1. Phillips & Wynne, carvers

London was a competitive place in 1848 with some 250 carvers listed in the trade directories. But as WGR's charitable works demonstrated, he was eager to promote the wellbeing of his fellow artists. Thus it is not surprising to find him coming out in defence of a respected London colleague who was complaining of plagiarism. Phillips & Wynne had agreed to provide a bread-platter to a London retailer, Felix Summerly, who had given it and the firm much exposure to promote his new decorative homewares catalogue. Appearing at the Society of Arts Exhibition, no less, in April 1848, it was reviewed by various high-profile publications.

The *Illustrated London News* even printed an engraving and wrote: 'The bread-platter is another useful domestic novelty: it is executed in wood, the rim ornamented with wheat, rye, barley and oats, designed by Bell, and carved by Phillips & Wynne; or the platter may have electroplated mountings, or be entirely of porcelain. The wooden platter may to the Londoner have a somewhat 'homely' appearance, but it is by no means uncommon at 'good tables' in the country: it will become whitened with repeated washing, and thus present that association of cleanliness and comfort which is so desirable in all table appointments'. Calling it a novelty must have irked WGR.

The Art-Union also described it as a novelty, adding: 'The design and execution of this object are both commendable. Wheat, rye, barley and oats, a very natural allusion to the purpose of the platter […] form the border; and but for their being somewhat "petite" for their situation, are, to our minds, just what the ornamentation of such an article ought to be. When produced in porcelain, the same design is hardly as effective.'

But the Phillips & Wynne /Summerly understanding turned sour when the self-same engraving (right) later appeared in a trade brochure printed by the Sheffield cutler, Joseph Rodgers & Sons, of which the firm claimed ownership. Felix Summerly had struck up a more lucrative relationship with Rodgers to produce a simpler version of the board, and thereby undercut Phillips & Wynne. However he did not update the engraving. Rodgers was in fact the very cutler who had

patented and produced the sweetcorn knife, also at the request of Felix Summerly (mentioned in the 'Thornhill' section above).

The Art-Union, which often served as a mouthpiece for artists, reported on the situation and invited WGR to give his views. WGR sympathised with Phillips & Wynne's grievance, emphasising that he 'has upon no occasion connected his name with the "Arts-Manufactures" of Felix Summerly, which comprise the platter from Bell's design executed as we have already said by Phillips & Wynne of Oxford Street [...] who did originally carve it and we presume do so still.' This may have been a veiled warning to avoid doing business with Felix Summerly.

Of course there was no protection for makers against plagiarism of their designs, but professional pride dictated that every artist in wood bring a personal spin to well-used motifs, to distinguish themselves from the competition. Thus Summerly's undisguised misattribution provoked a strong reaction.

2. Messrs Taylor, Williams & Jordan

Taylor, Williams & Jordan were machine carvers based in Lambeth, London. The firm had patented a wood-carving machine which was ground-breaking enough to earn a mention in a section of *The Book of Inventions* of 1848, entitled 'Sculpture by Machinery'. As the article pointed out, there were strong reasons why some manufacturers might favour these new machines over traditional hand-carving techniques: 'The cost of production by this process varies from about one fourth to one half that of hand carving; and the patentees, Messrs Taylor, Williams & Jordan…are prepared to enter into contracts, for the production of sculpture and carved decorations, of whatever kind, and to any extent.' The article goes on to say that 'the attention of Her Majesty's Government was drawn to the discovery', and consequently the firm won Pugin's contract for the Houses of Parliament interiors, churning out miles of oak panelling for the corridors of power.

Cheese Plate. The firm was also approached by Felix Summerly to produce a cheese plate (right) to add to his catalogue. The plate was reviewed by *The Art-Union*: 'We much admire a Stilton cheese stand, ornamented with appropriate subjects, among which are the cowslip, daisy, &c.' Despite working in a capital

CHEESE PLATE, in Carved Wood, with China Slab, 2l. 2s.

Cheese plate, Taylor Williams & Jordan, 1851. Courtesy Victoria & Albert Museum, London.

that boasted some 250 wood carvers, Summerly chose instead to go to Sheffield for the manufacture of his wooden goods, and, what's more, to a firm specialising in machine carving. The cheese platter was likely produced on a machine similar to the one patented by Jordan (below).

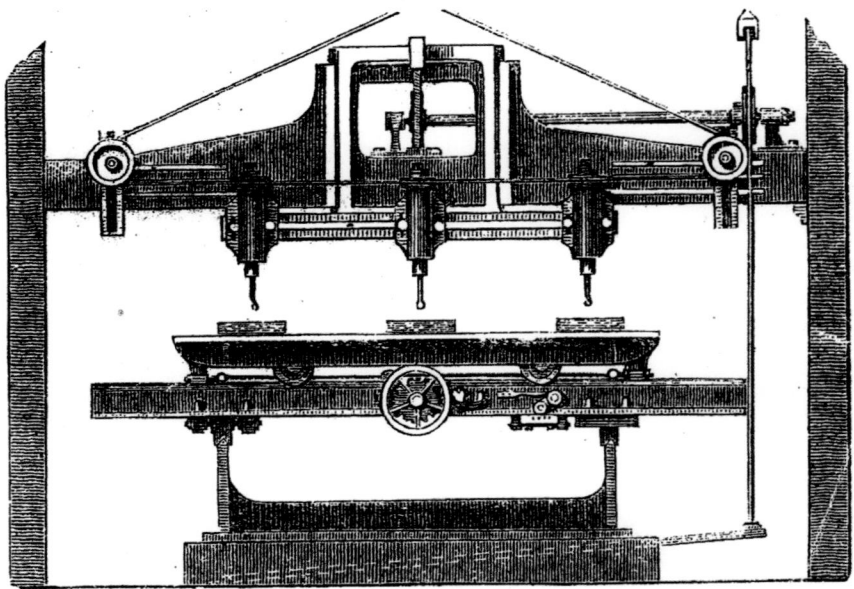

Jordan's wood carving machine, patented in 1845. From *The Art-Union*, January 1852.

Bread-platters. Taylor, Williams & Jordan also produced bread-platters such as this 'Waste Not Want Not' board (above right). The provenance is confirmed by a stamp on the reverse which reads: 'Jordans Carving Works, 154 The Strand.'

3. Felix Summerly, retailer, London

Felix Summerly was William Gibbs Rogers' most significant competitor, although not in terms of volume or skill or innovation. The greatest source of rivalry between them was for the attention of the Prince Consort, who patronised them both with commissions, purchases and awards. Summerly also got a bread-platter and a knife to market, and they were both illustrated in his new decorative interior goods catalogue of 1848. Each item was the fruit of a collaboration between celebrity artists, designers and manufacturers.

Third Time Lucky. Summerly's memoirs, published posthumously by his son and daughter in 1884, detailed the challenges of getting his bread-platter to market.

'Waste Not Want Not', by Taylor Williams & Jordan, sycamore, circa 1850
(Marie Lester collection).

In fact, it took three attempts before he succeeded with a commercially viable product: 'This bread-platter revived the use of wooden bread-platters or trenchers, and created a new industry still existing. Its history is worth recording. When John Bell's plaster model was sent to Sheffield, Messrs Rodgers hesitated to reproduce it, not believing that it would sell. They were persuaded to have one carved in wood. When done they fixed the price at £4 4s, which seemed prohibitive of a large sale. An essay was then made to have a platter executed in London, and it was proved that it could be sold for £3 3s, with a good allowance for distribution. This put Sheffield on its mettle: the London copy was sent to Sheffield, and after a short time a platter was forwarded to London by Messrs Rodgers, who stated it could be sold retail for £2 2s. From the year 1848 to the present time, the Summerly platter has been sold – besides innumerable other versions at the lowest possible prices; in fact, a new branch of industry was established at Sheffield, and, being easy of manufacture, at places more or less throughout the kingdom.'

First Summerly Bread-platter (£4 4s). At four guineas, this first version turned out to be too expensive. The carver isn't named but a trail of crumbs suggests it may have been William and George Wing of Sheffield (see the next section). Four crumbs to be precise. The first is circumstantial: Wing's descendants have a magnificent board, handed down through the generations, which may be the original that Summerly refused as being too expensive. The second is artistic sleuthing: an illustrated altar plate (below left) designed for Summerly by John Bell shows the same lettering as that of an 1887 George Wing catalogue (capitals 'B', 'W', 'L' and 'C' below right). The third is company legend: the Wing descendants' version of their firm's history, shared in the *Sheffield Telegraph* of 1935, states that theirs was the first company in Sheffield to turn plain chopping boards into attractively carved bread-platters. The fourth is high odds: between 1840 and 1852 there were less than a dozen carvers listed in the Sheffield trade directories.

Below: capitals from George Wing's *A Catalogue of Wooden Goods*, 1887. Sheffield Local Studies Library.

'Carved Wood Altar Plate'. P.13 from *A Catalogue of English Art Manufactures, Selected for their Beauty of Design*, 1853. Victoria & Albert Museum, London.

Second Summerly Bread-platter (£3 3s). Summerly presented this second bread-platter at the high-profile Society of Arts exhibition in April 1848, and described it as a 'novelty'. This was published in both the *Illustrated London News* and *The Art-Union,* goading WGR to go to his friends at the journal and set the record straight no less than three times. In August, the journal clarified that Rogers had been making these platters 'for many years', and would later refer to his platters as 'old friends'. The conflict between WGR and Summerly created a sudden spike of interest in what had, until then, been a quietly appreciated innovation, existing below the newspapers' radar. This second version is identical to the Phillips & Wynne platter, which Summerly may have bought or borrowed from the makers and later reused the engraving out of convenience, causing consternation among the carving community. (See 'Phillips & Wynne' above for the engraving.)

Third Summerly Bread-platter (£2 2s). Summerly states in his memoirs that he sent the three guinea platter back up to Sheffield to get a cheaper version produced, so this board (below) is likely to be a second Wing creation. It is very finely carved, and is on display in Room 122 of the Victoria & Albert Museum in London. It sits in a cabinet of Summerly pieces which are described as exemplars of 'appropriate decoration'. There are a few differences between the Phillips & Wynne model that appeared in the catalogue, and the two guinea version that was delivered to Summerly's customers. There is one quadrant less, meaning one ear of wheat less; the border is larger for ease of carving; the carving is all low-relief save one proud ear of wheat, to avoid risky under-carving; and finally the foliage is raised and doubles as 'ground', doing away with the need for laborious gouging and smoothing of the background.

Bread Board; limewood, with a carved border; designed by John Bell for Felix Summerly's Art Manufactures; made by Joseph Rodgers & Sons; English (Sheffield); originally prod. 1847, this example 1865. Victoria & Albert Museum, London.

The Summerly Knife. Summerly's bread knife (V&A No. 446-1865) was also designed by John Bell and manufactured by Joseph Rodgers & Sons of Sheffield. (See the 'Thornhill' and 'Phillips & Wynne' sections above.) It was offered with handles in ivory, boxwood, hollow silver and porcelain, and was reported on extensively in the press.

Cutting Remarks. The *Illustrated London News* described the knife in neutral tones, but *The Art-Union* plainly disliked it, describing it as: 'huge and unwieldy; and the ear of Indian corn, which forms the handle [is] a rather inconsistent application, for the grasp of such an object would, in the act of cutting, seem painful and dangerous. Even a simple roughed handle would be better'.

Novelty Value. Despite its description in the press, the bread knife was no more a 'novelty' than the platter was. A bread knife in Rosslyn's collection proves that the knife designed by Bell was inspired by an earlier piece. Knife No. 1, with a boxwood handle, is stamped 'WR', referring to William Rex (IV), 1830-37. Moreover, the flamboyant four-way curl-back of the silks (corn whiskers), and the experimental spatula-shaped blade are indicative of an earlier style. Summerly knives such as Nos. 2-4 were sold wholesale by Joseph Rodgers directly to Summerly, and to other retailers, and the handles were sold wholesale for cutlers to assemble.

WGR and the V&A. 'Felix Summerly' was actually the business alias of Sir Henry Cole (1808-82), who was instrumental in founding what would become the V&A, and who became its first director. Consequently, 'Summerly' is still honoured with his own display cabinet in the museum. It may be a coincidence, but the only acquisition representing the work of WGR is a small bracket, on show in the British Galleries opposite the Summerly cabinet. In a 1952 'Exhibition of Victorian and Edwardian Decorative Arts', WGR, for all his achievements, did not get a mention. By contrast, Summerly's work was exhibited in prime position.

Summerly/Cole Legacy to the Arts. Henry Cole was also instrumental in setting up the National Art Training School (which was renamed the Royal College of Art in 1896). Cole's programme prioritised the teaching of 'sketching', so designers ('creatives') could transmit their ideas clearly to makers ('technicians'). But giving priority to design at the expense of making had the effect of consigning makers to second place at best and anonymity at worst. Not being nurtured by the art establishment, makers lost prestige in the eyes of their clients, and their prices and profits were driven down, discouraging new recruits to their craft. Several artistic factions tried to swim against the tide, such as the Arts & Crafts movement of the late 1880s, and the Century Guild of Artists (founded in 1882, the same year as Cole's death), whose mission was to 'restore building, decoration, glass-painting, pottery, wood-carving and metal to their right place beside painting and sculpture'. But Cole's legacy came out victorious in the end, which perhaps explains why making is still considered less cool than designing, and why the Heritage Crafts Association has an 'Endangered Crafts List'. It remains to be seen if this present generation can revive the old concept of 'Designer-Makers'.

Cole's Legacy to Sheffield. The next section follows the trials and tribulations of William and George Wing, very possibly Summerly's uncredited turner and carver, who became the most famous and prolific bread-platter makers in the country.

George Wing

A direct connection between the Rogers and the Wings has not been uncovered, but they were both living and working within a stone's throw of each other in London, certainly in the 1820s and possibly through to 1840, and they both made a name for themselves making bread-platters. It is possible William Wing worked or trained at the Rogers firm in order to reach a level of carving skill as evidenced in his show board, illustrated below.

The Wing firm – father William and his three sons and grandsons – were one of Rosslyn's most exciting discoveries.

The Cornucopia board by William Wing, circa 1848, 16 inches.
Private collection, courtesy of Paul Freeman.

The Wing Look. Although we don't know what the Wing family looked like, we certainly know what their boards looked like. The lettering is mostly Gothic and the capital letters have distinctive bobbly serifs. Tom Samuel describes Wing's style as 'pragmatic virtuosity'. The Wings could carve superb pieces, but they were also savvy enough to minimise the time-consuming elements in order to offer a wide range of prices. This commercial approach came at the perfect time: the price of wheat had just been slashed by the Repeal of the Corn Laws and bread had become affordable again. Cobden's achievement was such a triumph for the downtrodden, that buying a breadboard was likely to be a charged political act, a defiant celebration of people power and plenty.

Career path

Early Struggles in London. William Wing (the Elder) was clearly struggling to survive 'in trade' as a 'chairmaker' in 1820s London. There was a mushrooming of industrialised workshops, and competition must have been fierce. He married young but his first wife died prematurely. His first two children, George and William, were born out of wedlock. Suffice it to say, it was in the midst of a bread famine, with destitution and the St Pancras Workhouse looming large. Some years later, he found the funds to marry George's mother, but again it was short-lived. By his third and final marriage to a Yorkshire lass in Rotherham in 1840, he had four children.

To Sheffield. William had relocated the whole family to Sheffield by 1840, and set up a turning-carving business with his eldest son George Wing (the Elder) as 'turner', employing four men and two youths. In the 1841 Sheffield trade directory, just four other 'carvers and guilders' are listed, so the business would not have been nearly as cut-throat as London. Leaving London proved to be an excellent decision, as WW's married life stabilised and three of his four children reached maturity.

The First Sheffield Board. It is claimed by the retailer Felix Summerly that he brought bread-platter making to Sheffield in 1847-48, although the carvers he used have not been recorded. It is our theory that Summerly and Joseph Rodgers & Sons used Wing, and this has been confirmed independently by a 1935 article in the *Sheffield Telegraph* about the beginnings of bread-platters in Sheffield: 'The manufacture of breadboards began in Sheffield about 1840…Prior to 1840 crude blocks of wood were used as breadboards, and it was a Sheffield chair manufacturer who in that year, conceived the idea of removing the primitiveness of the article by adding carving. Then followed the rounded board "turned" on a treadle lathe. Subsequently this was brightened by the addition of moulded edges, and the gradual addition of more elaborate carving, and other improvements developed the present day useful and attractive article.'

Summerly Connection. The date given in the 1935 *Sheffield Telegraph* article tallies with William's marriage in Rotherham and move up north 100 years earlier. More persuasive still, the 'chair manufacturer' mentioned reinforces the likelihood that WW the Elder was the first to make bread-platters in Sheffield, possibly years before they were approached by Summerly. If the Wings had been producing them with or for Rogers in London, they would have taken their expertise to Sheffield and would have been the obvious go-to for Summerly catalogue items.

Specialising. Also, Pigot's commercial directory for Sheffield in 1849 introduced a new section: 'Bread Platter Manufacturers', and George Wing was the only entry till 1860. No doubt every carver in Sheffield was soon to jump on the bandwagon as breadboards became a national craze.

Wing Virtuosity. It is circumstantial, but a strong coincidence nonetheless, that the descendants of the Wings still have in their possession such a superb board which was made at vast expense but never sold. It's possible that this is the first board which Summerly rejected in 1848 due to its high cost, is a close representation of the over-optimistic plaster model made by John Bell. That is why it remained at the Wing workshop and became their show board and a proud reminder of how the Wings turned their fortunes around. It is a mystery where William and/or George learned to carve like this. George also could have been in the employ of WGR before the move to Sheffield or some locally renowned carver. One of WGR's ex-employees did surface as a notable carver in his own right.

Cheap Bread. By 1850, the effects of the Repeal of the Corn Laws were making the country feel full and buoyant again. 'Punch's monument to Peel' shows Cobden looking on paternally as a family tucks into a whole loaf, with enough to spare for the cat. Although bread was readily available, long years of deprivation meant it remained something to appreciate, and what better way than to present the precious family loaf on some attractively carved platter. This jubilation, combined with increased disposable income, sparked a breadboard frenzy and Wing was ready to ride the wave with his prices for every pocket. In a strictly hierarchical society, breadboards reflected standing, in the choice of wood, the amount of carving and the size.

George Wing the Elder. By 1851, George Wing could afford to move out of the family home, 4 Burgess Street. He was established nearby as a 'Woodcarver', and listed in the census of that year as unmarried ('U'), with a year-old daughter, Emma (no birth certificate), and a 'Housekeeper', Emilia Berresford, who was older and apparently married ('M').

1851 Great Exhibition. In that very same year, no Wing is listed as exhibiting at the Great Exhibition, but William or George may have travelled to London and seen the boards of William Gibbs Rogers. Did they talk, compare notes, or discuss Summerly? Would the debate have been over artistic originality versus commercialisation? Did they do any distribution deals?

GW the Elder Takes Over. By 1852, George had expanded the business to an outlet in New Church Street, a central shopping street, as 'woodcarver' with his father and younger brother William Wing (WW the Younger) as 'turner'. His father took more of a back seat by this time and passed away in 1856, with the note: 'sudden death accelerated by drinking', and the two Wing sons carried on the business, now under the name 'George Wing'.

Platter maker. GW the Elder had a son, Walter, in 1858. On the birth certificate he gives his occupation as 'platter maker', confirming that he specialised even at this early stage, and that bread-platters had gone from niche status symbols to mainstream. Summerly is dismissive of such copycat platters, saying 'what follows must needs be inferior'. But in the same breath, he is proud his Arts-Manufactures business spread wood art to Sheffield. He can fairly be credited with lifting at least one family out of poverty.

F.W. Dover. In 1860, F.W. Dover joined in the competition for bread-platter making. Unfortunately, there are only a few items we can positively identify, despite the Dover pattern collection exceeding nine hundred items! An entry in *The Century's Progress: Yorkshire* of 1893 states: 'F.W. DOVER, Manufacturer of Bread, Butter, Eggs, Salt and Cheese Platters…This business, which has recently advanced with exceptionally rapid strides, was established 1860…Bread-platters are being introduced to vary the normal circular form, in new shapes, such as squares, octagons, &c…Mr. Dover has had a long experience of the class of business which he so successfully pursues, and much of the prosperity of his firm is due to the energy and industry with which he supervises every detail of the working of his factory.' The woods used for the platters were sycamore, oak and boxwood, and they were elaborately carved with fruit, flowers, leaves, wheat, barley and oats. Prices varied from 4d to £10 10s, with most being sold for between 2/6 and 6 /-.

Inside the workshop. The entry goes on to give a bird's-eye view of the firm's Sycamore Tree Works, situated at 114 Rockingham Street, Sheffield, with its workrooms spread over three floors, 'all fitted with the most improved modern mechanical appliances'. Dover started in Burgess Street in 1860, where William Wing also began twenty years earlier, but no prior working relationship is known.

Advertisements. In 1862, flush with profits, GW the Elder splashed out on a full-page, illustrated advertisement in Kelly's *Post Office London Directory*, which he kept up till 1874. Each ad included several engravings of his platters and a regularly updated array of accessories. The first breakfast tray appears in 1868. The images bear a striking resemblance to his 1886 catalogue, so it is possible there was an earlier catalogue. The firm expanded again, this time to Love Street. By this time Wing's fame had also spread as far as London, and, on the occasion of the International Exhibition, Kelly's *London Directory* noted: 'George Wing of Sheffield is known as the manufacturer of those elegant platters for bread and butter, which, carved in sycamore and other white woods, have added so much elegance and grace to the breakfast table.' Wing was joined by a second competitor in the same year, Samuel Duesbury, but no catalogue has come to light.

Breakfast tray, consisting of egg cups and dishes for salt, jams, marmalade, but missing the central dome for the butter, glass, sycamore, 12 ½ x 9 ¾ inches.

Electroplated platter with basket-weave insert, Wing, sycamore, circa 1890.

London agent. In 1871 GW the Elder, possibly with the assistance of his sons, found a London agent, Thomas Lavin, a 'house furnisher' of Bayswater, who may have provided the impetus for a first catalogue. I can't help wondering what WGR and his son GAR must have felt about their bread-platters going viral.

Upsizing. GW the Elder was also able to afford a gabled, double-fronted house, 7 Palmerston Road, in a leafy street in the suburbs of Sheffield, which still stands and is in private hands. Comfort and respectability at last. It was Rosslyn's dearest wish to buy the property and open a breadboard museum there to celebrate Sheffield's enduring legacy to our kitchen landscape.

London Outlet. To better tap the London market, Wing is listed in the London trade directory of 1874 in his own right under 'Bread and Butter Platter Manufacturer' and 'Bread knife Maker', with a 'fancy repository' at 84 Praed St, Paddington, still in collaboration with Thomas Lavin. It was but a short distance from his desperate beginnings at Pancras Street, Marylebone, where he was born to impoverished, illiterate, unmarried parents.

Golden Age. Lavin also opened up at 69 Cornhill, London EC1. The Wings were unstoppable. And there began the Golden Age. Meanwhile, back in Sheffield, they had more competition in the form of Henry Schofield, Stacey & Birch and John Wright.

Outsourcing. In London, a Thomas Doubble of 7 Bartlett's Buildings, Holborn, filed a Patent for an 'ornamental design for combination butter dish and egg stand'. A precarious concept, but a lovely example of the innovation phase when the output is most flamboyant. He had left nearly 40 years of haberdashery in Leather Lane behind, to reinvent himself as a 'Manufacturer' and was still a going concern till 1882. Wing was his maker.

Family concern. In 1879, the Wing dynasty consisted of George and his four sons: 'George Wing Snr, Manufacturer of bread and butter platters and wood turner, Plane Tree Works, 10 Sycamore St.; George Wing Jnr, General wood turner, 12 Sycamore St.; Walter is noted as a woodcarver and commercial traveller; his third son William, became a 'cutler manufacturer's clerk' and no doubt looked after the financial side; finally Alfred Wing, 'Wood bread-platter and bread knife manufacturers, Silloth Works, 65 Division St'. This small, burgeoning family concern was the typical business model seen in Sheffield.

Punch drunk. The whole family must have got a kick out of seeing 'On a Bread-Platter' in *Punch Magazine,* dated 24 July 1880. *Punch's* cartoon lampooning sub-standard education for the populace, showed a mother trying to teach her son how to read the words in Gothic lettering running round the border of the family bread-platter. Hot on the heels of this endorsement came a number of trade awards.

Silver Medal, NZ. It is extraordinary to think Wing was shipping items off to the Antipodes for Trade Fairs. The first was awarded in 1882 from an Exhibition in Christchurch, New Zealand in the form of 'First Order of Merit, Silver Medal' for 'Bread, butter and cheese platters, breakfast and egg trays, bread and butter knives'.

Exhibition Pieces. The Cornucopia and Basket-weave were exhibition pieces, which is confirmed by their great size – larger than the standard 12-inch boards – and extra-special carving. They could be considered as being in the style of Grinling Gibbons, in that they are naturalistic, deeply carved with a lot of high-risk under-cutting. They would have been exceptionally expensive to produce and would have been hung on the walls of the firm's offices to impress new clients. These two boards appeared in the 1882 Wing catalogue, so it is possible they were the medal winners. They tended to be stained dark and polished to look like mahogany, as light-coloured wood was still associated with the kitchen and practicality.

Cornucopia

For Exhibition. Mentioned in the previous section, it may have been refused by Summerly as being too expensive, and would have initially been a great disappointment for Wing. However, it is likely it repaid the time and cost amply, being shipped around the world to gain renown for the company at industrial exhibitions, like the one above. It is a virtuoso performance showcasing under-carving so adventurous that the petals are entirely off the ground, anchored only by the flowers' receptacles. This board reappears on the frontispiece of the second Bramhall catalogue, after Wing was bought up by them in the 1920s.

For Sale. Just as at a fashion show, no one expects to wear anything they see on the catwalk, but the designers translate certain elements into something practical for daily use. Following the same principle, the catalogue version is simplified and stylised, with a lower-relief (shallower) carving. It's a smaller board and a fraction of the work, with a narrower border. There are fewer motifs and the ones left are more symbolic. The overall trend towards simplification may have been equally driven by cost-effectiveness, and by changing tastes created by the Arts and Crafts movement.

Cornucopia board, catalogue version, sycamore, 11 ½ inches.

Silver Medal, London. More accolades came in 1884 as George Wing was awarded the Silver Medal in the London International Universal Exhibition, Crystal Palace Company, for 'Carved bread and butter platters'. The global competition would have meant this was a grand achievement. There must have been a selection Committee. One wonders who won the Gold Medals. These certificates were still hanging in the company offices when Rosslyn went to visit. We cannot be sure what he won them for, but his early catalogue of 1882 provides another possible candidate.

Basket weave

For Exhibition. In a private collection by descent, this basket weave board is one of five known examples in platter format, and does not appear in the later 1886 catalogue. They must have been a popular earlier model, suggested by their size

Basket weave exhibition piece. Private collection, courtesy of Paul Freeman.

and lavishness, but may have been dropped due to expense. This also becomes the poster board for the Bramhall catalogue.

For Sale. The basket weave examples in the 1886 catalogue are also platters, but the weave is broader and the border has the flavour without the virtuosity. One such is bordered with wheat and rye, and interspersed with overlapping wild flowers.

Although they are not listed in the catalogue, Wing also supplied basket weave inserts to silverplate makers, as five of his known pieces appear in combination with ornate bread salvers (see page 191). Sheffield was experimenting on all fronts – with different combinations of materials, colours, textures and shapes.

Wing basket weave board, catalogue version, sycamore, 11 ¾ inches.

Poppies and wheat

For Exhibition. This board (below) does not appear in either of the catalogues with this combination of elements, but every motif, including the ribbon and acanthus, are Wing signatures. It would have been kept in the 'Best Office' to impress prospective customers.

Poppies and wheat, Wing exhibition, fruitwood, 14 inches.

For Sale. The poppy and wheat catalogue version (right) appears in combination with agricultural tools, including a scythe, sickle, beater, fork and rake. The pea pod is also a rare element. On the catalogue board, the poppy is similar but the exhibition piece is far better tooled, with deep over-curling leaves. The poppy heads are bent back with the thin proud stems curving over delicately. Truly masterful.

Poppies and wheat, Wing catalogue, sycamore, 13 inches.

Vine, Wheat and Hops

For Exhibition. This has the feel of an early Wing piece that has been converted into a mirror, quite crudely, we assume by the owner. Despite the crack which occasioned the need to upcycle, the carving is in great condition. One explanation is that the wood had not been seasoned properly. A breadboard usually contains both heartwood and sapwood. The sapwood is fresh growth on the outer part of the trunk and contains more moisture or sap; the heartwood, at the centre of the trunk, is dead and drier. The two woods shrink (lose moisture) at different rates, and, if not seasoned slowly and long enough, will result in splitting.

Vine, wheat and hops breadboard now a mirror frame, sycamore, 15 inches.

Vine, wheat and hops, Wing, sycamore, 13 inches.
Private collection, courtesy of Paul Freeman.

For Sale. There is little undercutting, but this would have been sold as a high-end board, predating the catalogue. Grapes, wheat and hops cover most alcohol types, and would have pleased a Tippler. We can associate this with Wing, as it has impeccable provenance. There are three known examples, suggesting that they were made for high-budget customers, but didn't warrant inclusion in the later catalogue. The collection example measures 13 inches, suggesting an earlier creation.

'Cut and Come Again'. This is another Wing exhibition piece which does not appear in the catalogue, although Wing offered simpler boards with the same motto. A deep-carved piece, it expresses a strong sense of movement as the wheat spirals round the border, untamed by the lettering which, on other boards, can break the momentum with their radial lines if the wheat is less dominating.

'Cut and Come Again', Wing, sycamore.
Private collection, courtesy of Paul Freeman.

Two Exhibition Knives. These are very finely done and largely unused, with wheat and barley motifs on either side. Most handles had a carved upper side and plain lower side. Both blades are stamped with George Wing's name. He would not have needed to stamp his own blades, as generic blades (as shown in the catalogue) were cheaper. But for exhibition he would have gone to the trouble, ordering a minimum of a hundred to get the stamp. This was one of his investments in advertising and the pieces may have been entered in numerous trade shows, even across the world.

Wheat and barley exhibition knives, boxwood handles, blades stamped 'G. Wing'.

The 1886 Catalogue. Riding high from these achievements, he published a second catalogue in 1886. Alongside F.W. Dover, with his offering of nine-hundred items, Wing's fifty pages of wooden tableware may have been among the largest choice of bread-platters in one place in the country. The two Wing catalogues are quite similar, but the later version dropped the show-stoppers, possibly because the sales were not justifying the space. Equally, the standardisation to a round foot in diameter meant less room for highly ornate carving. It is a step towards commercialisation and practicality. The following section showcases a selection of the finest items in the collection, which appear in the catalogue.

Trends. Fashion was moving from the very elaborate to the simplified. The later boards are not inferior because they are simpler, they are more refined in a way because they are a happy medium between the self-expression of the carver and the practical needs of the user not wanting to feel anxious about snapping something off every time the board was used. The role of the breadboard evolved from a precious status symbol at the breakfast table, to a robust working item that people used in the kitchen and the dining room everyday for cutting everything on. There was a synthesis of essence of wheat with minimal effort. The aristocrats probably all had one by then and carvers sensed a whole new market was opening up as more kitchens were being built with somewhere for the board to sit. Equally, the growing knowledge about bacteria from the 1840s and the focus on maintaining hygiene may have been a key factor in the demise of the deeply carved, extravagant boards.

Knives

Wing's knife handles are arrayed over three pages towards the front of his catalogue. His handles appear in the collection married with blades bearing other cutlers' marks, so we know Wing supplied the cutlery trade. Mr Hawley remarked how the collaboration had to be very close to produce a beautiful result: 'The skill in knife making is the balance – when it's on the table it should balance on the holster, the blade should not touch the table. They drilled a wire down the handle to provide more counterweight if necessary.' Where the handle and blade connect harmoniously, the carvers and cutlers have collaborated, as in knives No. 2-4. Wing would have overseen the project with a local cutler. Where Wing sold the handles wholesale to cutlers around the country, the blade and handle makers could not collaborate, and a displeasing mismatch of size, weight and shape often resulted, as in knives No. 1 and 5. The collection contains many such examples. One tell-tale sign was the addition of a ferrule to disguise the unhappy marriage.

Miniature Bread Knife. Again stamped George Wing on the blade, it is an unusual piece for its short handle and bird-knife blade. It is possible he had a line in children's sets, and found this cheaper solution, rather than especially made mini-bread knife blades. There is also a miniature bread knife made of a small handle saying 'BREAD' affixed to a butter blade.

Box Set. Behold a beautiful example of an almost unused box set with a bread knife and matching fork, which does not occur in the catalogue. The special packaging suggests a wedding gift, which could have been used to cut the wedding cake. Wheat can be approached in innumerable ways, so the workshops identified themselves by a house style. In Wing's case, the top tip of the ear of wheat points away from the blade. Even following the prescribed pattern, every carver added his own subtle distinctions. 'Every chisel mark is an aesthetic decision', according to Tom Samuel.

Ferrules. The difference is very noticeable when Wing has overseen the assembly process. Wing never used ferrules on his own knives in his catalogue because he would have made sure all the components fitted snugly. Where the blade stamp is identical to the catalogue – marked simply 'Bread Knife' – it is assumed these were assembled in-house in Sheffield.

Bread Fork. These were not for toasting, but for transferring slices tastefully from the board to the plate without touching them. The silver plate has similar bobble-features to other silver-plated items in the catalogue.

Bread knives. Among the selection, knife No. 5 throws up a number of interesting possibilities due to its early London blade. Made by Weiss of London, it is marked 'VR', but similar in shape to another earlier Weiss blade marked 'WR', dating it to William IV (1830-37). Did Wing supply these handles to Weiss before he moved to Sheffield? Or did Weiss originally employ Wing in-house? Did Wing work in Rogers' workshop and supply Weiss? Did Wing take this pattern with him to Sheffield – a bit of artistic plagiarism – which would make this particular handle originally somebody else's?

Napkin rings and salad servers

Wing was constantly expanding his range of items and materials. In 1862 he patented the idea of a wood-glass combination in a general-purpose dish. By 1882 we also see a plethora of sycamore and oak tableware, married with silver-plate,

a selection of which is illustrated below. The use of oak makes detailed carving harder and was fashionable, especially the darker colour of the rings. There were many ways to darken wood with chemicals such as nitric acid, ammonia and darker polishes.

Cheese platters

Ferns are a fun idea, delicately executed, and with a shell at the bottom. There are also many teapot stands, kettle stands, cigar ashtrays in a similar wood and porcelain combination, with many choices of carved motifs, matching other accessories, so clients could buy entire matching sets.

Butter platters

Butter platters (below left) were also available to match your bread-platter. The shallow, moulded blue glass liner, which has a textured bottom, protected the wood from the butterfat. This example is in immaculate condition, very deeply carved with an orange, peach and grapes, surrounded by their individual foliage, alluding to marmalades and breakfast fruits. Individualised butter dishes 4 inches across and salt cellars also appear.

Biscuit jars

With its original clear glass barrel (above right), the wooden base display wheat, barley and foliage, and the top is playfully formed of an ear of wheat.

Egg stands

Egg stands were an attractive addition to Wing's breakfast accoutrements, with built-in egg cups that lodged securely in the tray. Offered in various shapes and sizes, they catered for the individual with a 2-egg model, up to a 6-egg tray for sharing.

Bread-platters

The vast majority of goods were bread-platters. Space only permits a selection of Wing's offering to be showcased here, chosen for their variety.

Key (all boards made of sycamore):

1. A rare board with a range of fruit, very deeply cut, but very worn, 11 ¾ inches.

2. A rare fruit board with pears and strawberries, the blossom in tandem with the fruit, 12 ½ inches.

3. Three overlapping dog roses, wheat and barley, combined with ivy for friendship, with a central symmetry, showing how Wing mixed and matched motifs, 12 inches.

4. Square boards were unusual, the overwhelming preference being for round, and are reminiscent of Tudor trenchers. It is less wasteful of wood and is also practical as it would not roll about. The corners are decorated in opposing flower/leaf and wheat/bud designs within renaissance strapwork, 11 inches.

5. Oak and leaves, very stylised, a cheaper board to make, shallow carving, clearly popular as Bramhall continued this model. Finished with oil with a nice patina, in good condition, 12 inches.

6. The very stylised berries and leaves pre-empt the trend towards simpler patterns in the 1900s. Relatively cheap to make, the standardised 12 inch size suggests it was made later. Unused.

7. Wing has added 'BREAD' within a stylised ribbon, in Gothic lettering, his signature 'B' with a teardrop shape in the upper bowl, combined with oak sprigs and ivy, likely a later model, 12 inches.

8. Given its larger size (12 ½ inches) this suggests it may be an earlier board. Wheat, oak and acorns are carved symmetrically, the leaves pointing out and in consecutively. The blonde colour is due to much scrubbing.

Key (all boards made of sycamore):

1. A fabulously busy board displaying very small apples and pears, which is unusual for Wing, not carved to scale, accompanied by acanthus, wild flowers and buds, wheat, rye and even wild grasses, 11 ½ inches.

2. 'Waste not Bread the Staff of Life' is a bumper motto which is most often seen separately, as Bread / Waste Not / The Staff of Life. The carving has been saved as the owners have preferred to use the reverse, causing a considerable depression. It was a popular line, for the more moralising customer.

3. Earthenware dish, 'The Staff of Life', 12 inches. The patterns on this earthenware bread dish are pure Wing down to the last detail, even the flapping ribbon, and proves he made models for the potteries, as did WGR. Surprisingly, this exact phrase does not come from the Bible, although 'the staff of bread' is mentioned in Leviticus 26:26, when God threatens to 'break the staff of bread', in other words, 'to cut off the main support of life which is bread'. It seems the Irish writer Jonathan Swift (1667-1745), is to be thanked for the phrase. In *A Tale of a Tub*, a satire on the English, his hero Lord Peter, gushingly declares: 'Bread…dear brothers, is the staff of life, in which bread is contained inclusive the quintessence of beef, mutton, veal, venison, partridge, plum-pudding, and custard.'

4. 'Spare Not' with wheat, barley and leaves, a light-weight model, suggesting it is later, to use less wood. It keeps the best features of the earlier ones without detracting too much, but it is more industrial and less artistic. The Arts and Crafts Movement preferred simplicity and it may be reflecting this change in public taste, but Wing was too perfectionist to go down the William Morris route completely, 12 inches.

5 'Take Freely and Thankfully', a joyful invitation to share, with a moralising after-taste, has Wing's signature flamboyant capital letters and a full stop to help the reader find the start and finish. These motto-only boards have a textured background, by using a punch with different designs, called a stipple. Common shapes are stars, crosses, rows of dots, circles and lozenges. This was done to darken the background and raise the profile of the lettering, 12 inches.

6. A salver, decorated with leaf sprays, the twigs forming projecting handles. The patent dated 1862, shows Wing was the first to combine wood and glass in this way. He must have been confident it would be a good seller, and took the trouble to invest in protecting his idea. Again it is unusual in that the leaves project beyond the edge, making the design more fragile, and thus was likely used more for buns and pre-cut slices, 12 ½ x 11 ½ inches. The insert has been lost.

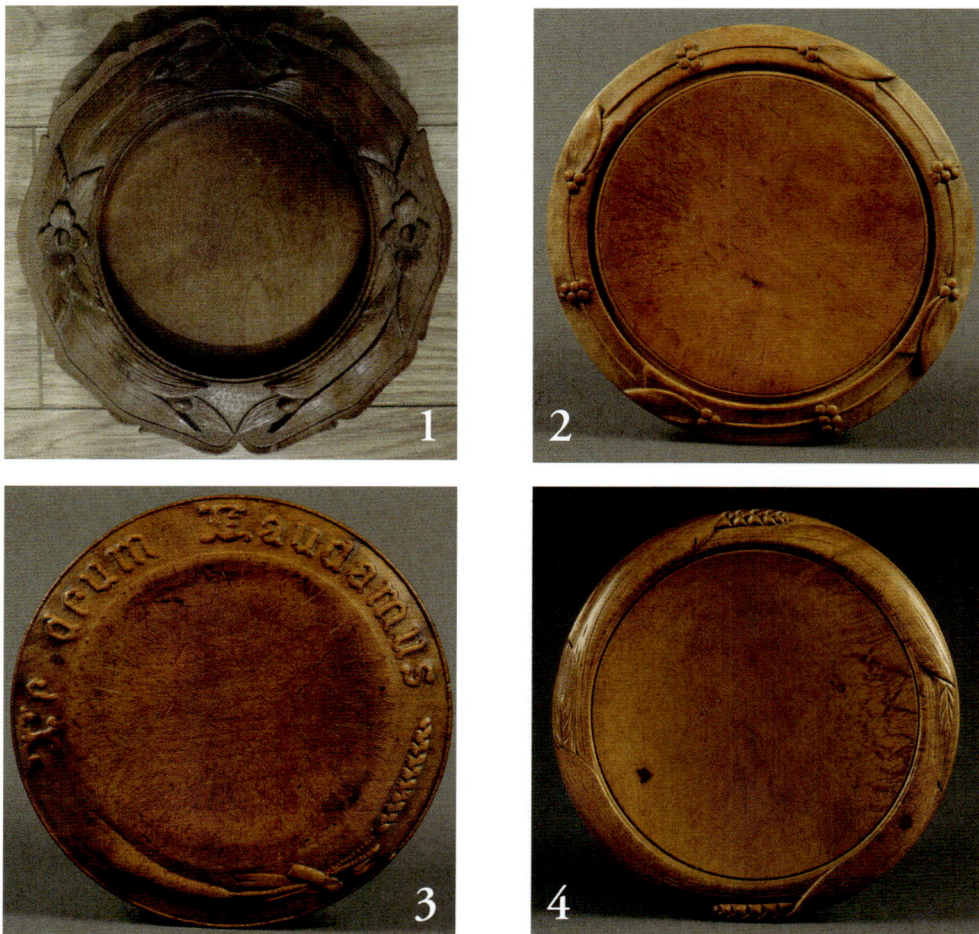

Key (all boards made of sycamore):

1. A dish decorated with flowers and leaves, chosen as an example of his scallop-shaped edges, shows a diversification from breadboards, the curved bowl suggesting it didn't have a liner and was used for dry food items such as nuts and small fruits or rolls, 10 inches.

2. A rare stylised laurel, a later board, simplified and cheaper to make, 12 inches.

3. 'Te Deum Laudamus'. Unusual as a Latin Board, 'We praise you Lord', and is the beginning of a famous Gregorian hymn dating from the 5th century. A number of composers have set the words to music. It would have been the perfect gift for a devoted Christian, or a Vicar for his altar, 12 inches.

4. A simple, stylish platter, with two wheat and two barley ears opposed, the ground of foliage in low relief, allowing speedy production and low cost price. The medullary rays which transfer nutrients across the trunk are especially fiery and attractive, 12 inches.

Special commissions

The following section contains all the one-offs we can identify through Wing's signature carving. A certain leeway has to be conceded as to dates and attribution because Bramhall bought Wing in 1920 and inherited its carvers and its house style. There was a transition phase in which it is impossible to tell which company made which board, until the Bramhall style eventually became more defined.

'Presented to Gertie by Cousin Walter'. The message on this board is charming and has sparked much lively conjecture among museum visitors. We know it's a late Wing board, so Cousin Walter had it custom-made by the foremost bread-platter maker in the land. There are many letters packed in, making it an expensive gift, as customers were charged by the letter. It celebrates her 21st birthday, when she would get the 'key to the door', and could get married without parental consent. So was Walter staking his claim? It is usual to inscribe the name of the receiver on a gift, but somewhat overbearing to immortalise yourself with your name. Initials on the back would have sufficed. Imagine the moment at Gertie's big party: did she rush into his arms or shrink back in embarrassment, her friends tittering into their kerchiefs? The fact that Gertie never cut a slice of bread on it in her life means she either proudly displayed it or hid it in a cupboard. Ha! Note the quality carving, such as the detail in the flowers and the compact lettering. It is the best work, and a lot of it, on a blemishless bit of wood – a good example of how a board looked and felt the day it was made. Sycamore, 12 inches.

'**Don't Skin the Loaf**'. A large armorial commission, the escutcheon personalised with a bird, one leg up in Ministry of Silly Walks-mode. Wheat and poppies spray out naturalistically on either side. An unusual feature is to carry the foliage on around the lettering, requiring a wider border. It is possibly an earlier board due to its large size; it certainly looks impressive but is not deeply carved. The back is stamped with 'Lund, Maker, Cornhill, London'. Lund was a very reputable company famous for making high quality vanity boxes, sewing boxes and corkscrews, whilst also specialising in ivory carving. Lund also produced some exquisite bread knives. But this is a Wing board which Lund must have ordered. The typography is unmistakable, sycamore, circa 1800s, 13 ½ inches.

An interesting aside. The meaning of the motto has intrigued many a visitor. Some wondered if it means, 'Don't serve a thin slice', i.e. be generous with the portions. Tom imagined it meant 'Eat your crusts', an unpleasant proposition in those days when the ovens were heated with logs and were full of embers and smuts, which would stick to the dough, leaving it hard and blackened. Barbara, a museum visitor, observed that the Cornish did not use to eat the outside of a pasty for that reason. It was treated like lunch-box packaging and discarded. As another aside, to remove the unsightly, unpalatable burnt portions, a special tool called a 'bread rasp' was designed, which appears in Timmin's Catalogue.

'**Sweet is the Bread of Contentment**' (above left). This sounds like a Bible nugget, but its origin is unclear. It is a call to moderation at table. Sycamore, 12 inches.

'**The Earth is the Lord's**' (above right). The carver needed to abbreviate the original to fit it round the board. I imagine some discussion ensued with the client about aesthetics and cost and practicalities. The phrase comes from the first line of Psalm 24: 'The earth is the Lord's and the fullness thereof'. Sycamore, 13 inches.

'**We Eat to Live not Live to Eat**'. Summarising with good humour the fundamental difference between the French and the English; whereby the French live to eat. A perfectly spaced motto, with Wing's signature curlicues on the capitals and full stop. Sycamore (Mikki Towler Collection).

The Demise of George the Elder. By 1888, George the Elder employed 12 men: quite an operation, considering how it all started. The 1891 Census lists William Wing the Third as 'Cutlery merchant's clerk' as before, Alfred as 'cutlery traveller', Walter as 'woodcarver' and George the Younger as 'woodturner'. George the Elder passed away in 1897. In his Will, he stated 'I give my tools and machinery to Walter and William' (the carver and the number cruncher), 'and the good will of my business and £300 to put into the business if they decide to carry it on in partnership. I desire my sons William and Walter continue to employ my son Alfred as Traveller in the same manner that I now employ him.'

Changing Tastes. By 1902, Sheffield boasted only three bread-platter manufacturers: Wing, Dover, and Church. It seems the heyday was drawing to a close. It is not clear what caused bread-platters to lose their decorative vava-voom. They became smaller and the carving very simple, basic even. It is what people wanted; plain and cheap. Why tastes changed so drastically around the turn of the century could be down to many factors: the end of servitude, Socialism and the fight for workers' rights, skills and wood shortages during the Boer War, or Trade Union fair-wage campaigns. Despite the turbulent backdrop, in 1907 Wing's customers included Army & Navy Cooperative Stores, which must have been a great boost for business, with Empire-wide exposure, although the Wings were not credited.

Dover Buyout. A long-standing competitor cum collaborator, Dover had been successful enough to buy the freehold of Sycamore Villas in Eccleshall Rd and its land. But the firm finally succumbed to financial pressures. By 1911, Wing and Dover had merged, which explains the two bedraggled sheets with a Sycamore tree logo given to Rosslyn. By chance, Rosslyn collected a few of his boards and knives.

The small selection of Dover knife handles shows his style to be Art Nouveau, especially the lily. His motifs are in a bigger scale compared to Wing.

St George's Cross, a popular motif, with a fern pattern, Dover, sycamore, 11/12 inches.

'Bread', the magnified wheat border is notable, with a Wing-style 'B', Dover, sycamore, 11/12 inches.

Bread on a ribbon, the half-flowers poking out being the carver's signature, Dover, 11/12 inches.

Breadboards were sometimes transformed into paintings and hung on the wall, Dover.

Decline and Fall. The new 'bread plate' was in demand: cheap, easy to store and quick to wash. It may be the Wings were stuck in the Victorian age and did not adapt to the times quickly enough. Or the family had burnt out, the grandchildren not willing or able to carry it on. But a pair of brothers who had 'obtained their early knowledge of the business with the old firms of G. Wing and F.W. Dover', launched their own breadboard business with a difference.

Bramhall of Sheffield 1909-2002

Just as Sheffield had turned into the cutlery hub of the world, so it was for breadboards, thanks to the tireless efforts of George Wing. Bought out by Bramhall, the tradition continued apace, as Bramhall flooded the country, and the Empire, with affordable breadboards and bread-knife handles. It made sense to stick near the cutlers. Boards and knives went hand in glove, the patterns on the one echoing those on the other. Dozens of specialists, 'Little Mesters', all worked independently and collaboratively on the different stages of the production process, to deliver in vast quantities the unassuming board-and-knife sets we remember today.

Defying the Odds. Through the 1900s, the Great Depression and two World Wars created great turbulence across communities and businesses. Although some employees may have been too old to go to war, recruiting the young afterwards must have been a challenge. Their customers' disposable income would have defined the value, irrespective of the time and effort put in. There were highly skilled carvers in-house, proved by their one-off creations, such as Queen Elizabeth's Coronation board (see page 102), but the demand was mostly for cheap products. The only way to respond was to make the carving simpler. Bramhall developed a low-relief style with extensive use of veining to give the ground some texture.

Chain of Command. Established by the Bramhall Brothers at Rodley Lane, the firm was inherited by the Haynes family and then taken over by Mr Whewell, 1982-2002. And with it ended the story of breadboard manufacture on a grand scale in Sheffield. Mr Haynes, the last but one MD, pronounced it 'Bram-hall, the posh way', when answering the phone, although the Sheffield lane of that name is locally pronounced 'Brammul'.

Quintessential. While Wing and all his competitors passed into obscurity, Bramhall came through it all as the last man standing, redefining for the 20th century what most people identify as a quintessentially British breadboard.

1909-1910s

Founders. 1909 marked a watershed as Aquila Lemon Bramhall and his brother George Frederick, 'practical craftsmen and experienced throughout the trade' set up their own company. Aquila Lemon – a name chosen by his mother who 'was reading some novel at the time' – became commonly-known as 'Quil'.

Still life with popular Wing/Bramhall breadboard, by E.H Parionage, oil on canvas, 1915.

Leaders. Despite the decline in ornate boards, Bramhall became the leaders in the new market. The firm brought fresh impetus to the industry by correctly reading what the new century wanted: simplicity, practicality and affordability. A lesser-known branch of Sheffield's industrial output, they widened their advertising reach with a splash in the *Great North Magazine,* where they proudly introduce their improved technology and large staff. They offered worldwide shipping capabilities to Australia, South Africa and Canada.

Publicity. There was clearly an image problem Bramhall was trying to unpick. 'These goods are so thoroughly domestic that we are likely to imagine that they are made by carpenters and other woodworkers as a "side-line"'. With carving becoming more simplified, Bramhall sets itself apart: 'Their work has a unique beauty in its fine carving and finishing, quite unapproachable by any other maker'. The ex-Wing carvers 'whose…elaborate workmanship on some of the finer work is really an accomplishment of art', continued certain of the old lines which were more ornate. It is often not possible to accurately date the models which appear across both companies. Ex-Wing items appear in the Bramhall section of this book if the carving showed subtle signs of simplification.

Massive Output. They publicise 'an attractive catalogue in the form of a booklet', lightweight and easy to distribute, offering a much more limited range, and making the carving more 'suggestive'. Their tone is upbeat and go-get, rearing to take bread-platters into a new full-on-commercial phase. They boast of producing 5,000 bread-platters and 3,000 butter dishes weekly!

1920s

Merger. Bramhall bought out Wing in 1920, inheriting the show boards, prize certificates, carvers and house style. Their publicity uses the Wing heirlooms on the frontispieces of three early catalogues. The basket weave offered by Wing was continued on by Bramhall. The weave effect was difficult to get right; keeping the lines straight and the depth even were the greatest challenges. Mr Haynes in 2003 remembers: 'You would see basket weaves being worked out and discarded in the workshop as people had a go and lost it'. Mr John Thomas Clarke specialised in these lattice effects and died in 1963.

'Foolish Possessions'. While the stacks of boards visible in the photos are round, there were rumblings of dissatisfaction with the old ways. The writer below may have been expressing a general disaffection since bread sizes had outgrown the round Victorian 12-incher, which had been designed originally for a cottage loaf. 'Certainly I have always felt that breadboards are among our most foolish possessions. The ornamental edgings and carvings catch crumbs and butter, and need infinite patience in scrubbing to keep them clean. A round board is usually a foolish choice: there is no place to balance a heavy bread knife and there is no means, the carved edge sloping off, of preventing the crumbs from scattering elsewhere. Hence the frequent use of a pastry board (which should never be scored with knives) or a tea cloth which does not benefit by the addition of margarine and cuts.' *Daily Herald*, 21 May 1923.

Going Oblong. It did not go unnoticed, for the Bramhalls were publicising their all-new oblong breadboards certainly in the 1930s. In the likeness of pastry boards, they better suited rectangular loaves, and even came with convenient knife slots. In fact, many designs for housing the knife snugly were patented.

Catalogues. The firm published numerous trade catalogues, which are a wonderful way of assigning provenance, as none of their boards were signed. Too numerous to reproduce in their entirety, there follows a small selection to whet the appetite and give an overview of the wide range of styles and prices on offer. None of the catalogues are dated, and that was intentional, to avoid yearly reprints. Decades can only be estimated based on printing styles and stylistic clues. Many lines repeat across Wing and through Bramhall, others are discontinued, yet others are introduced, sometimes with patents.

Cheap Vandyke. This is the nickname for this board with a scalloped border, according to the pattern book kept by Mr Harry Haynes in the 1930s, with additional outer petals.

Van Dyke board, Bramhall, sycamore, 12 inches.

'Waste Not'. Identical to the catalogue illustration, it is more expensive and rarer.

'Give Us This Day Our Daily Bread'. An innovative Bramhall design, as far as we know, but the lettering follows the Wing style.

'Waste Not', Bramhall,
sycamore, 12 inches.

'Give Us This Day Our Daily Bread',
Bramhall, sycamore, 12 inches.

Special Lines board, Bramhall, sycamore, 12 inches.

Special Lines Board. Another of Bramhall's quintessential breadboards, carved with 'Bread' in Gothic script, a rosette and leaves. It was a hugely popular model.

Special Lines Knife. An ornate bread knife with wheat and flowers, some peeping out from behind the wheat, it appears also in the Wing catalogue. The blade is etched: 'The Grafton Bread Knife Patent 15685', with an unusual three pronged tip for skewering the slices and offering them round safely.

Special Lines Knife (above) and an illustration from the Bramhall catalogue (below), showing the 'Special Lines' range of boards and knives.

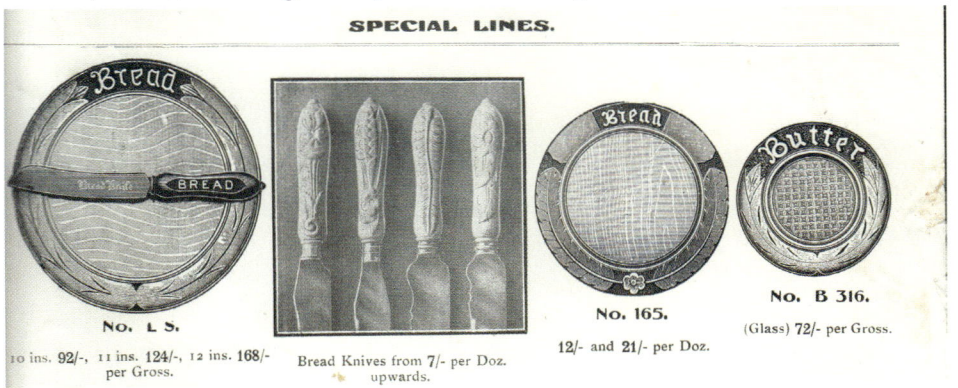

Bramhall's Artistic Woodwork Brochure. The brothers produced a second catalogue, proclaiming their yearly participation in the London Board of Trade Exhibitions from 1916-20, and containing a few pages of breadboards. They present themselves as an 'Artistic and truly British Industry', their prices ranging 'from a few pence to a few pounds'. The business even included drying sheds to season their own timber. While appearing dominant, the reality was less predatory and more collaborative. According to the numerous brochures showing breadboards made by other companies, some even in the same 'works' or building, the designs seem to be very similar, so if one firm got a big order, it shared the work out.

Company Ethos. The firm's ethos was presented in the brochure: 'Concentration is our motto – and concentration means greater production. We are the largest makers of Artistic Woodwork in Sheffield and our works are solely given up to its manufacture.' Unfortunately, their Rodley Lane works 'burned down to the ground' due to a gas lamp accident, so they moved to Mary Street and started from scratch.

'AB & LR Long Life and Happiness',
sycamore, 12 inches.

'Long Life and Happiness',
worn bare from use, circa 1930,
sycamore, 12 inches.

'AB & LR Long Life and Happiness'. A later Wing wedding board, this does not appear in his great 1886 catalogue, but in a separate, undated six-page pamphlet. With bells and a horseshoe, these boards were made off-the-peg or personalised. Note the initials, 'AB' and 'LR', for which the customer would have paid more. It seems that breadboards carved out a niche in the trousseau market. Worn but cared for, this board suggests a successful marriage! It may have been kept for best as the reverse is unused. It was a popular line, with four known examples.

Compare the fate of a similar board after multiple generations of marriages. While most chattels followed patrilineal rules in terms of inheritance, it was usual for the breadboard to be handed down through the maternal line, the eldest daughter having first refusal. Maura, our Irish neighbour, confirmed this custom. A number of guests have expressed their regret when this unspoken rule was broken: if a breadboard enshrines mother-love, then it is not surprising for daughters to wish to cherish it and not let it out of the fold. But the problem comes when there are two daughters…

Talking of which, two sisters, Bridget and Janice, visited the museum and brought with them their ageing parents' Bramhall breadboard, sent by express delivery from their father's home in the Isle of Wight, especially for the occasion. They were clearly close and the unmentionable question was 'Who would inherit the breadboard?' At the end of the tour, one sister found the For Sale box and fished out a 'sister board', identical down to the individual chisel marks in the word 'BREAD'. It must have been made by the same carver. They were both overjoyed and bought it forthwith.

Two Barley, Two Wheat, Wing /
Bramhall, sycamore, 1930, 12 inches.

Wall flowers. Wing/Bramhall, oil and
plaster on sycamore,1920s, 12 inches.

Deco flowers, sycamore, 12 inches.

Ivy weave, sycamore, 13 inches.

Two Barley, Two Wheat. A Wing (Cat. pp. 44-62) inheritance, it was continued as it was simple and lightweight, the leaves seemingly twisting freely in the breeze.

Wall Flowers. The same board as above, but after cracking in two – and being far too charged with memories to throw away – the owners mended it by screwing a piece of pine to the reverse and embellishing it with an 'impasto' (raised) painting of a cottage and garden. It was retired to the parlour wall, no doubt.

Deco Flowers. Inspired from a Wing piece, the Victorian foliage has been stylised and simplified to suit an Art Deco taste.

Ivy weave. Also a Wing inheritance, it includes wheat, barley and flowers, but again simpler, in a pleasing Art Deco style, keeping abreast of the art trends.

'Our Daily Bread'. An all-new Bramhall model, it was seemingly very popular. It must be noted that catalogues were not indicative of what was made, as goods were only made to order. Despite the simplified lettering, the signature capital 'B' with the upper bowl in the shape of a teardrop still appears, a respectful nod to their Wing forbears. Mr Hawley said catalogues were platforms for showing off, and many objects were never made. The lettering has lost its blobs and is more curvaceous, requiring fewer tools and gouges, and the foliage appears in a new layout.

'Our Daily Bread', Bramhall, sycamore, 12 inches.

'God Bless Our Home', Bramhall, 1933, sycamore, 11 ½ inches.

1930s

'God Bless Our Home'. Dated 7 June 1933, this is a custom-made wedding board, personalised with two sets of initials, 'EB' and 'WFB', with a one-off motto.

Four Sheffield Makers. By 1934, there were four breadboard companies: Ashby, Bramhall, Burrell, and Church – though Peter Dowsett, a carver at Bramhall, when interviewed in 2001, said that Ashby was a middleman, not a manufacturer. The *Leeds Mercury* of April 1935 writes: 'Kitchen brights have vanished from the domestic scene and bread-boards bid fair to follow suit. Still, wooden bread-platters still have their place in many homes.' Despite this downbeat observation, Bramhall reported impressive sales the following year.

4,000 per Week. In 1935, Bramhall got the endorsement of 'our Trade Commissioner' in the *Sheffield Telegraph* of 29 November. The generous article included photos of a turner and carver. The latter, Mr Jack Blackwell, was a legend in the firm for carving all the intricate jobs. The term 'bread board' was used instead of 'platter', signalling that somewhere between the turn of the century and the 1930s the simplified carving no longer justified the word 'platter', and that 'board' had become common parlance, as its practicality was more important than its aesthetics.

Founder. Interestingly, the *Telegraph* article also claims that breadboards started off in about 1840 in Sheffield, which prompted our theory that William Wing may have been Summerly's contact through Joseph Rodgers in 1847-48. Company legend has it that the innovator was 'a chair manufacturer', which ties in with William Wing's own description of himself on the birth of his first son George in 1820 in the St Pancras Parish records. As an aside, when Rosslyn made this discovery at the London Metropolitan Archives, she noted: 'Amazing coincidence. I could have hugged the girl who read a very dark entry in the Baptismal records. I drove home on a high'. The article continues: 'Prior to 1840, crude blocks of wood were used as bread boards.' The founder is credited with 'the idea of removing the primitiveness of the article by adding carving'. As previously mentioned, the Wings hailed from St Pancras, only a 30 minute walk from Soho, where W.G. Rogers had his workshop. So it is possible the families had met or worked together before and even after the Wings' move to Sheffield.

Success Story. It is notable that their 1912 off-the-peg output of 5,000 breadboards per week has reduced to 4,000, using up 700 sycamores per year. Despite this, the Bramhall brothers are upbeat, creating 'demand to such an extent that more bread boards are being used to-day than ever before'. They are proud of their heritage, keeping certain popular models from the Wing catalogue, but also introducing innovative designs such as 'the oblong bread board with knife slots at the sides'.

Winchester. The residents and visitors of Cathedral and University towns also had a penchant for boards, as 'mementoes'. Where local carvers were not able to satisfy the market for oak souvenir boards in tourist hotspots such as Winchester and Canterbury, Bramhall was supplying oak boards with mottos such as 'Manners Makyth Man' or 'From Ancient Winchester'.

Souvenirs. Marks of Winchester was a silversmith that attached its silver Winchester Cross and Trusty Servant to Bramhall products. The 'Arthur boards' were carved in oak by Mr Clarke, 'an artist'. 'He could carve all the Knights' names if you wanted.' They would be fumed in ammonia to darken them. Bramhall would also arrange for them to be repaired. It is difficult to attribute each item for sure, as local carvers were also supplying the souvenir retailers.

'From Ancient Winchester', Bramhall, breadboard turned into a
three-legged stool, oak, 12 inches

Winchester Stool. Bramhall's pattern archive contains a rubbing of this very
model, 'From Ancient Winchester'. This example has been cut on, before being
competently converted into a stool using three broom handles. It is shallow-carved,
with a 30 shilling price tag. The lettering is broader, but Bramhall kept the look
and ribbons of a famous Winchester carver, Laverty. (See 'Laverty' section below.)

Bramhall Manners. Bramhall was making Winchester souvenirs reminiscent of
the old square trenchers into the 1980s. A kind donation to the museum by
Bramhall's descendants shows the development of Bramhall's style, with lighter,
curved lettering instead of the square look. The engraved scrolls are well balanced
and steady, while the armorial chip-carving is detailed and accurate.

Loyalty Boards. The article also confirms Bramhall was getting commissions for
'token boards…in enormous quantities', which were part of loyalty schemes used
by companies both related and unrelated to baking, although none are mentioned
by name. (See the 'Advertising and Promotion' section for more information.)

Clients. From the 1930s-50s, other clients included Army & Navy stores, which had been customers of Wing. They were also carving many one-offs for clients, such as a rude one involving a bull, for presenting to a slaughterer! Welsh-related boards with 'Bara' or sightseeing place names were despatched to Wales for the tourist market.

'Ymenyn' ('butter') dish, accompanying a 'Teisen' ('cake') board, with matching leeks and the Prince of Wales' feathers, oak, 10 inches.

1930s Pattern Book

New Lines. Harry Haynes, chief carver, began his pattern book in the 1930s, with 1937 noted as the final date. It provides a wealth of insider information about styles, customers, prices and tools. His designs were coded 'H' for Haynes and the numbering runs from 1-303, so he was quite prolific. He worked alongside his turner Mr Coates, who was also given instructions in many captions. The trends included painting the borders, black and orange in some cases, new oblong shapes, new mottos such as 'Salad', slots for the knives and 'sketching' with a V-tool rather than deep carving. He created integrated cheese and butter boards, all with matching slot-in knives – the big new thing. He mainly used sycamore, but some oak boards are also on the books as well as one chestnut item.

Customers. The pattern book lists the customers by many of the patterns, suggesting some clients wanted a specially designed product, made uniquely for them, rather than off-the-peg. Bramhall delivered far and wide to retailers and the cutlery trade, including the famous Sheffield cutlers Wostenholm, Allinson's the bread maker, John Lewis, and the London Co-op.

Gothic Folly. As a breath of fresh air from the piece-work, totally original orders came in, such as a 'brown oblong' with 'Spire Handle, oak' requiring creativity and artistic sense. These one-offs were carved by Fred Kitchen, one of their prize carvers. Mr Kitchen and his colleague Mr Blackwell were often absent on ecclesiastical restoration projects for lofty York Minster and Lincoln Cathedral no less.

French Market. 'Framage' and 'Buerre' boards were made for 'Printom' – presumably Printemps, the classy French department store. Another French 'Hors.d.oeuves' tray and even a square 'PAIN on ribbon' board appear, proving again that English manufacturers were carving in French for the French market. Fragmented records such as this, where a French retailer used an English maker, suggests that decorative breadboards were not intrinsic to French culture.

Coronation 1937. The final year of the pattern book being 1937, Bramhall does not fail to offer a variety of Coronation boards to mark the occasion. Rather than carving, they chose red and blue paint. 1936-7 saw a constitutional crisis caused by Edward VIII refusing to give up Wallis Simpson, which led to his abdication. It would have been unclear who was going to be King when these boards were being stockpiled, which perhaps explains their lack of wording. One example reads: 'V-tooled lines, painted 2 colours, Red outside. Blue inside, middle part left plain, also knife.'

Knife Slots. The accompanying knives were a special feature, matching closely or exactly the pattern and colourways. Most often, Goodlads is mentioned as the cutler, which Bramhall eventually bought up. He also filed patents for designs which housed the knife more securely. The notes read: 'Special oblong for Gills, New patent exposed knife.'

Vertical. Whereas the carving had always been on the horizontal, they experimented with the vertical, an idea carried on by Oak & Rope today. The notes read: '3 in 1 Specialty turned, carved block letters, straight up carving.'

Family Recollections. Frank Hastings wrote in response to an advertisement Rosslyn put in a local paper appealing for information about the family with a great anecdote: 'My mother Mabel Hastings had a cousin, Quiller Bramhall [*sic*]. She was born in 1900 and lived in Sheffield all her life. When I was about 13, say 1937, she took me to see a lady…who was packing breadboards in a warehouse. Was she Quiller's wife? My mother remarked to me that her breadboards came from there. We had two, and one had a head of wheat carved round the rim with the words "WASTE NOT WANT NOT". We went down the Moor and the place was between there and St Mary's Road.' Packing breadboards I know about, from helping Rosslyn on her stalls. It's back-breaking work.

Wholewheat. 'Wheat all way' has a more Deco feel, getting away from the naturalistic, towards the stylistic. It is deceptively simple, as the spacing is challenging, and involves 200-300 cuts. The carver has achieved the uniformity of a machine, but by hand. On the practical side, it would make a good crumb catcher due to its generous gully. A modern take on an old motif, the continuous band is more relaxing on the eye. It is not in the catalogues and was probably a one off or special line.

Wholewheat, one of my favourite boards, sycamore, 12 inches.

Artistic Woodware Brochure

Another catalogue came out with a yellow, green and black cover, reminiscent of a 1930s look. It is not a sure indication of the 'make-date' of a breadboard matching these images, as catalogues were kept for years, decades even, and the items could have been carried over from earlier catalogues which are now lost. It is only a snapshot of what was available.

One Good Turn. Bramhall introduced this new line, which retains the natural patterns of barley and wheat, harking back to earlier boards, but takes them to a new level of abstraction. The carving covers only ½ inch, and the rest is turned. The turning is elaborate with lots of ins and outs, and is decorative in its own right. Turning is quicker, but still skilful – and it is more cost effective to give the turner more of the work. It adds good crumb retention to its list of benefits, alongside being easy to clean.

One Good Turn, Bramhall, sycamore, 11 ½ inches.

Turners. Mr George Coates and George Farrell, from the 1930s, deserve a mention. The turners are also very skilled in getting the rough-sawn blank of wood perfectly shaped and smooth, ready for carving. Their enemies are knots, which need to be found and navigated with the minimum amount of wood waste.

Octagonal. The feathery effect of veining on the leaves gives texture without depth. It might have been bought specifically for painting on, as the border conveniently doubled as the frame. It continues the Victorian hobby of painting on 'white woods', as evidenced by George Wing's catalogue which provided a whole page of items including frames and stools. The artist is very skilled and it would have never been used for cutting bread. David Haynes commented: 'There was danger money paid for squares, octagons and ovals. 1d extra per board.'

Serrated Bread Knives. The discovery of stainless steel in 1915, so trumpeted by Sheffield as the end of the 'daily grind' of knife care, was received by customers

Octagonal. River scene, oil on sycamore, 12 inches.

with little enthusiasm. It was not as hard as carbon steel and thus users objected that the knives did not sharpen or cut as well. 'One of our cutlery workers said stainless would never catch on', recalls a Haynes family member. So Sheffield responded by bringing serrated edges to the table.

Serrations also took a long time to be accepted, as the major objections were: you can't sharpen serrations and serrations ruin the knife sharpener. They also shredded clothing. The company announced how serration: 'has increased the sale of bread boards by killing the housewife's old custom of carving a loaf when resting it against the body'. The Bramhalls saw another opportunity to increase sales. With every new breadboard came the slogan: 'Use a Bread Board and Save the Tablecloth'.

Bramhall Knives. A selection of Bramhall-like knives from the 1930s, show how they started by carrying on the Wing patterns and then in the 1930s, narrow blades and serrations became the fashion.

A selection of 1930s bread knives, sycamore and stainless steel, serrated edges.

Packaging. Bramhall knives came packaged, the yellow one slightly earlier, but the script is mostly similar. The grey example has a hard-sell blurb on the back. 'Cut your bread the modern way' and 'This knife will also cut icing without cracking and is useful for lemons and tomatoes'. The trend was back to multi-purpose. The grey packaging also states: 'The knife has a special type of fine teeth arranged so that the knife cuts both when pushed forward and drawn back'. The two knives are unused, one wrapped in greaseproof paper.

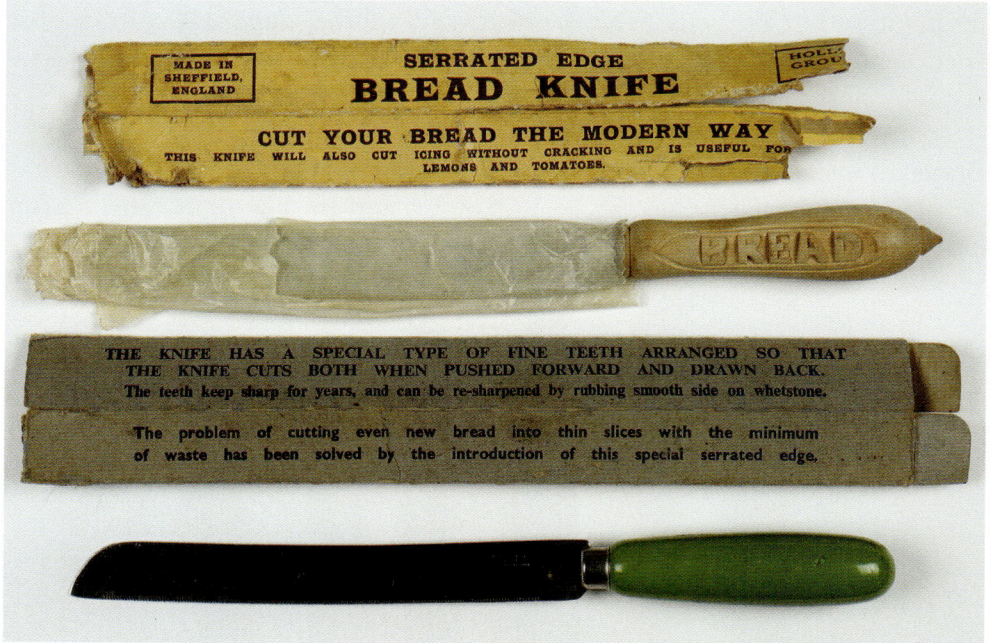

Bread knives with 'cartons', sycamore and stainless steel, card, 1930s.
The green painted handle was one of a series of colourful alternatives which were all the rage in the 1930s.

1940s

Army Boards. The Second World War drove another innovation. To satisfy the MoD contract for chopping boards, Bramhall took to joining slats together, with tongue and groove and glue, as materials were scarce. The factory was inspected and the boards were stamped with the Ministry's number. Such methods have now become the norm with some retailers only guaranteeing their products for one year, because of instant splitting and warping.

M&A. By 1944 there were more amalgamations. Burrell, Holland & Co. had incorporated Church and Ashby. The Bramhall archives contain a Burrell brochure, but it is not clear if Burrell staff were eventually merged into Bramhall.

Burrell Octagonal. Burrell Holland was an example of another good maker, but despite their proximity to Wing, they had original ideas. For example, Wing's octagonal is embellished with leaves.

Octagonal flowers, Burrell breadboard, sycamore, 12 inches.

Burrell, Holland & Co. of Sheffield. The Sheffield trade directories mention various companies over the two centuries, mushrooming and fading out. Burrell, Holland & Co. was one such, incorporating Church & Ashby, at Emu Works, Eyre Street, before fizzling out in its turn. Among the newly discovered Wing archives, appeared a two-page trade brochure which helped attribute two more items in the collection.

235

Burrell Ferns, sycamore, 11 ½ inches.

Burrell Ferns. Again, like subtle signatures, Burrell's fern tips meet, whereas Wing's bypass each other in opposite directions. As a general trend however, all the companies involved in batch production and paying workers piecemeal were moving towards a simpler, low-relief style to maintain profitability.

Down Your Way. In 1949 David Haynes, Harry's son, joined the company. Mrs Bramhall chose David to run the company, which he did until 1982. He may have been instrumental in getting the company onto a Home Service edition of *Down Your Way* with Richard Dimbleby featuring Mr Jack Blackman and the workshop. His chosen song was *Under the Spreading Chestnut Tree*!

Pokerwork. David Haynes remembered in 2003: 'During the war, poker work was all the rage, so my father (Mr Harry Haynes) would bring blanks back home and with the poker machine, which he still has but is in need of repair, decorate the borders. My mother did the painting.'

1950s

'**Long Life and Happiness**' **to Her Majesty the Queen!** (see page 102). There are three examples known and it may have been a popular board. The SS looks remarkably Germanic, in the zeitgeist of the time. An elaborate board, dated 2 June 1953, the carver is having fun and showing what he can do. A joyful sense of celebration is evident as the carver takes a break from the standard lines. Clients wanted to pay more to mark an end to austerity and a new age of peace and optimism.

The Sheffield Star. In October 1956 the company got another helpful plug from the *Sheffield Star.* Interestingly, this article still advertised their oblong boards as if they were a novelty.

Rosslyn was being offered round breadboards in considerable quantities from the 1980s, possibly because everyone had upgraded to oblong boards and their old round boards were surplus. The new shape was no doubt driven by the larger rectangular loaves. Many guests at the museum ask if 800 g packs of sliced bread weren't the worst thing for breadboards. But I hear anecdotes that boards became buttering-stations, placed next to the toaster, and were also a perfect size for processing two slices simultaneously during sandwich-making.

As well as shapes, the firm experimented with xylonite for knife handles, but it was found to be very flammable and was discontinued.

Oblong (Artistic Woodware Brochure 3–H42), sycamore, 12 x 10 inches.

1970s-1982

Eventually, by 1970, Bramhall was the last man standing. Their second Mary Street works was luckily recorded in photographs in 1980 by Annette Humpage, a member of the family who played an important role in the business, especially in the Finishing Warehouse. Annette and her brother Tony Haynes, are the last descendents of the Bramhall line to have experienced working in the firm, and generously shared their archival photos and reminiscences to give a taste of what life was like inside their firm. We can assume it was pretty typical of other workshops.

Family concern. David, who took over from his father, Harry, was a very pro-active manager, mucking in with all stages of the process. He did anything from weighing the boxes for delivery to sharpening the serrations. He found the progression from low-relief carving to engraving a shame: 'It's not proper carving, it's scratching'. But it was what the customers wanted and could afford. And it kept the company afloat, when much of Sheffield was in decline.

Workforce. The workers were almost like family, sometimes staying their entire lives in the firm, even well into their nineties. They had to be very strong to carry stacks of breadboards up and down the wooden stairs to the next stage, piled higher than their heads!

Working with wood. Wood dust hung in the air, making you cough, and settled in the rafters making a fire hazard. It was not an unhealthy atmosphere as it was all natural substances. Tony mentioned loving the woody smell, except when they got some foreign timber called afromosia instead of walnut, which smelt like pepper, and had them all sneezing. Nothing was thrown away. The shavings were sold to a piggery and stables, the sawn-off corners went for firewood, or were used in their stoves. But there was lots of unusable wood because of imperfections such as knots and splits. If the blemish was small enough, the piece could be sold as 'seconds'. 'You'd hear the expletives flying if somebody found a knot.'

Sycamore. It was the perfect wood, being strong and having no taste. Also, sycamore has a tight, close grain and better resists moisture. Bramhall also made washing dollies 'peggy-leggies' out of sycamore and other household utensils for this reason.

The Site. Annette drew a very precise map of the three cramped storeys of the U-shaped building, and provided some precious photos, taken soon before they closed as a family firm. Combined with the lively anecdotes, they give a gritty, atmospheric glimpse of the inside of a breadboard maker's. It was a well-oiled process, honed over generations, and sheds light on just how many stages there are and the huge effort involved in getting a board and knife ready for sale.

Decline and Fall. Already in financial difficulty by the late 1970s, David Haynes broke with tradition and advised the younger generation not to join the company. The end was inevitable because the items were designed for durability, so eventually the country would become saturated with them – there was no need to buy new ones. David bankrolled the firm, trying different strategies to keep it afloat, but it was eventually closed down in 1982 'by the accountant'.

Salvage Operation. In that year, the family salvaged what it wanted from the building before the new owners took over. The contents of the large safe in the corridor, never locked but with the key in the slot, more anti-fire than anti-theft, were saved. There the model boards were kept, and the old Wing pattern books from the 1880s. Thankfully, we now can refer to the illustrations made by Wing and Bramhall, and identify the makers. But many precious company records were lost. 'It didn't seem that special for us, it was just life.'

The Tools. Tony saved the tools in a munitions chest. He was very knowledgeable about the machinery. The old way was a generator which turned one long axel up high, punched through multiple rooms. It was sufficient to engage it with a strap to use a buffing wheel, grinding wheel or lathe. They then modernised the plant with self-contained motors. Workers' desks all faced the windows to use natural light. The U-shaped building gave all rooms access to daylight. They did use gas lamps, but they were dangerous.

1982-2002

New Management. The site was cleared by Terence Whewell who took it on with the old staff, and kept English sycamore breadboard production going another twenty years. It was during his stewardship that Rosslyn visited the firm with boxloads of boards for identification. In the 1990s, Rosslyn found a very reduced staff.

Windmills. Peter Dowsett identified her windmill as one of his from the 1950s. They started on the round and then branched out into different shapes, keeping the carving low-relief but creative. He was also 'recarving' old boards, where the customer wanted to give the worn pattern a new lease of life.

Windmill board, sycamore, 12 inches.

Exhibition. Rosslyn was allowed to photograph one of Dowsett's exhibition boards, made for a display at a Chatsworth show in 1986, with the motto 'Bramhall Woodware Ltd'. He must have sold a few, without the motto. It's lively, big and bold, with a feathery effect, created by much chip-carving, and uses short veining to suggest leaves.

Worn tools. When Rosslyn observed that there was no music, no background noise, just hammering all day, Dowsett had answered: 'Hammering hammering – that's ok – thut's munny'. Rosslyn also loved tools and noticed he had: 'the most worn mallet with deeep [sic] indentations from the ends of the chisels, to the point that the corners are almost worn through to meet each other'. He had four different stamps or 'stipples' for punching into the ground.

Branded Logo. In the 1980s-90s a branded woodpecker appears on breadboards, framed with lines in the shape of a 'B'. New colourful brochures were produced showing off-the-peg lines. Customers were even provided a form with blank boards

Peter Dowsett's exhibition board, sycamore, 1986, 16 inches.
Private collection, courtesy of Paul Freeman.

to sketch their personalised designs. This is the modern version of the archetypal breadboard, with cursory chips to suggest foliage to try and give movement, requiring only one spin of the board. Tom estimated it would take 2-3 minutes to chip out the BREAD, using four chisels at least. Despite making shortcuts with the carving, the firm always used prime sycamore without joins for their breadboards and cheese boards, making their products very robust: boards made in the 1990s will last hundreds of years. The chopping boards, however, were made of slats glued together and gradually chopping boards replaced breadboards altogether. The process began in the 1960s, made possible by the development of slow-degrade wood glue.

Simple. In 1991 the Sheffield *Telegraph* announced that Bramhall is 'carving a specialist niche' in the kitchen utensil market, after buying up a firm which produced dog combs. MD Terence Whewell's optimistic tone disguised the fact that the business was clearly in decline, as the very trend they benefitted from seventy years earlier was taking 'simple' to a new level, one involving absolutely no carving at all.

241

Peter Dowsett's exhibition board, retail version, sycamore, 1986, 16 inches.

2000s

In 2002 when Rosslyn visited again, she got the distinct impression the firm was struggling. 'The boards and knives aren't selling. The turner retired and the carver was on two days a week, only carving if there was an order. No apprentices.' Another possible reason for the decline, according to David Haynes, was a culture in which 'Older carvers would not teach the young ones'.

From the 2000s 'Handmade, hand-turned' breadboards were seen as an unnecessary expense, as over-harvesting also meant sufficiently large sycamores had become rarer and more expensive. Cheap replacements in the form of plain, multi-purpose, glued-together 'chopping boards', sourced from Eastern European and SE Asian forests were the final nail in the coffin.

That very year they ceased production of breadboards and turned to garden furniture. Mr Dowsett and Mr Eades, who had been part-time for some years, retired and thus ended an era. In Britain at least.

Till the end, Bramhall remained loyal to their heritage of making breadboards from the choice cuts of the tree, that would endure the daily wear and tear of a working kitchen for hundreds of years, if well looked after. They stood by the optimum, quintessentially British product, perfected over at least 200 years by our artists in wood. As the age of plastic draws to a close, demand for durable domestic wood-ware made of one well-chosen, well-seasoned piece of sycamore might just make a come-back.

Laverty and Samuel

Thanks to Rosslyn's investigations and irrepressible enthusiasm, two other workshops of the 1900s can be showcased here. Both were in the conservation business, but Laverty also carved prolifically for the tourist market, while Samuel, still carving today, appeals to a niche clientele.

James Thomas Laverty. Laverty took over the restoration of Winchester Cathedral from a Mr J. Thomas, who appears in a trade directory of 1877 as 'carpenter and joiner'. The records show Thomas briefly restoring the cathedral interior from 1878 to 1886, using 'oak 1000 years old'. His workshop very likely produced breadboards, though they are not mentioned in the Cathedral's restoration log. Laverty arrived in Winchester in 1878, and may have worked with Thomas, before starting his own company. Between 1892-1915, Mrs Kipling's card

'Manners Makyth Man', sycamore, 13 inches, retailed by Mr Savage.

index of restoration work notes 'Thomas & Co.', a partnership between Laverty and his architect partner Mr Kitchen.

Laverty specialised in the ecclesiastical side, including carpentry, woodwork, church furniture carving, turning and cabinet making. According to his obituary 'he carried out much beautiful oak work in churches and mansions in many parts of England, including Winchester Cathedral, the College and the Church of St Cross'. This may explain why most of the Winchester boards celebrate these three institutions. In 1892 the firm is noted as using 'old wood' so the repairs would be in keeping, but it is only belatedly in 1906 that the records confirm them as using old oak to make pilgrimage souvenirs. Where the oak is ancient, we have assumed the boards were made between 1878-1920, deriving from the nave roof and foundations etc. Although we have no visual evidence, the ancient oak combined with the admirable ecclesiastical carving are strong indicators. The firm carried out all the conservation work on Winchester cathedral till 1953 and the family became a local institution. Laverty, while dominant, was not the only firm supplying souvenirs.

'Oak Taken From Winchester Cathedral Nave Roof 1086-1896', possibly made by J. Thomas, from ancient oak, 13 inches.

Cathedral Cornucopia, possibly by Thomas & Co., ancient oak, 12 inches.

The Laverty Sons. By 1915, J. Thomas Laverty Snr had been joined by some of his eight sons and the company was renamed Laverty's. A trade directory of 1921 has them listed under cabinet makers, upholsterers, carpenters, joiners, carvers, guilders, warehousers and carpet dealers, and in 1941 as antique dealers. Respondents to Rosslyn's appeal for information in the *Hampshire Chronicle* described the family as 'the Cathedral carpenters', 'excellent wood carvers' and 'antique restorers'. The four Winchester institutions that made it to the board were: the Cathedral, William of Wykham, the Hospital of St Cross and King Arthur.

'Oak taken from Winchester Cathedral Nave Roof 1086-1896'. Strangely, the dates don't quite match. Bishop Wakelin started work on the new cathedral in 1079 and consecrated it in 1093. Daniel, a church architect who visited the museum, thought the 1086 date had been massaged to make it more 'symmetrical' with 1896. The lettering is of square incised capitals on a floating ribbon, trimmed with star stipples. The Cathedral's coat of arms appears at the top, a shield with the keys of St Peter, Gatekeeper of Heaven, to whom the cathedral is dedicated alongside St Paul, represented by the sword.

Cathedral Harvest, oak and silver, 12 ½ inches.

Cathedral Cornucopia. Showing the harvest bounty with a wealth of motifs, this board features shallow carving, as oak splinters easily. Our forester could tell from the grain that the 'tree was not thriving, because the growth rings were densely spaced in one place. But when a neighbouring tree was probably coppiced, the tree had a growth spurt, indicated by the subsequent rings appearing further apart!'

Cathedral Harvest. Local silversmiths often worked with carvers, embellishing boards with silver ornamentations. But silver is not an ideal material to add to a cutting surface, suggesting that the boards were intended more for presentation or display than use. However, this oak board, laden with fruits in low relief, has a central silver shield decorated with the arms of Winchester which is much damaged by knife cuts, so it has clearly been used. The board is of two pieces of wood, either due to splitting or because the carver ran out of large enough beams. A stamp on the reverse reads: 'D. Frost, The Square, Winchester'. Frost appears among the jewellers and silversmiths of Winchester in certain trade directories of 1877-86.

Beechwood souvenirs, possibly carved by J. Thomas, 1906, oak, 8 x 8 inches.

Beechwood Souvenirs. Incredibly, the medieval monks had simply laid layers of logs, like a vast raft, across peat bog, by way of foundations. There is some confusion as to which wood was used. A contemporary article mentions beech, which is noted for its durability and strength, but is susceptible to rot and insect attack. Internal Cathedral restoration records kept by Mrs Kipling show Mr Thomas made 'articles, beechwood from foundations' for sale at his outlet in Cheesehill Street, with 'Proceeds to fabric fund'. However, this oak dish has the following inscribed in ink on the reverse: 'XI cent oak taken from foundations of Winchester Cathedral during renovation by Sir Francis Fox.'

Winchester College and William of Wykeham. Many other boards commemorated Winchester College, founded in 1382 by William of Wykeham, Bishop from 1366 to 1404, who shares his arms and motto with the College. It is not clear why the boards favour Wykeham so unanimously over the 101 other bishops. Wykeham's blazon is 'argent two chevrons sable between three roses seeded or, barbed vert'. Rosslyn heard from an old Wykehamist that there is an argument that Wykeham didn't have an official coat of arms and made it up. He therefore had no right to give it to the College. This might stem from the fact that the College of Arms was not set up till two years later, probably to stamp this sort of thing out!

Wykham Square. A luxury model in the shape of a Medieval trencher, beautifully carved with the floral insignia of the UK, and two coats of arms, raised instead of engraved, the reverse with 'AWR Christmas, 1905' and bun feet.

His motto, 'Manners Makyth Man' is less about manners and more about customs or 'ethos', being translated from the Latin 'mores', and very telling, as his college created a unique set of customs which all the boys had to live – and even die – by. It was by some accounts a gruelling experience, the memory of which made even elderly Wykehamists shudder. Nothing was made easy. Pupils as recently as the 1950s were using square wooden trenchers, a usage dating back to 1416, when they are first noted in the College purchases as 'disci lignei'. Hilary, a Brother of the Charterhouse, London, informed me the Scholars still eat off wooden trenchers, as a badge of privilege. Another Wykehamist, Mr T. said he used to put his mash in a circle round his trencher and everything inside, so it wouldn't fall out, as the central depression was always too shallow. By coincidence, he was taught woodworking and carving by the very same Austin Laverty as made the Winchester boards, and that was his happiest memory of the whole place. Makyth or brakyth.

Wykham Square, newly felled oak, 12 ¼ x 12 ½ inches.

Knocker of the Trusty Servant, brass, 5 x 2 ½ inches.

Servant Knocker. 'Sweating' was Winchester College's equivalent to 'fagging' at Eton, where a younger became the servant of an elder. The original mural, miniaturised on this breadboard, can be found in the Buttery, outside the College kitchen. The composite animal with a boar's head and a deer's hooves has a whole story behind it. An accompanying poem in Latin and English describes how each feature represents the attributes of the perfect servant. It is my suggestion that this mural was a form of teaching aid, used by the older boys to instruct the younger ones about expectations.

Trusty Sweater, lacquered oak, Birmingham 1907, 12"

Trusty Sweater. The lettering is squeezed onto the narrow ribbon, but with very successful acanthus leaves, with silver inlay. The motifs also served as teaching prompts to transmit our heritage to the next generation, but not always with the greatest success. A guest to the museum recounted how she never asked what 'Manners Makyth Man' meant, next to the Trusty Servant on her parents' breadboard, but developed a theory of her own: a mad scientist called Manners must have made a Monster-man, in the style of Frankenstein!

The Hospital of St Cross. Winchester also had a long tradition of using wooden plates called trenchers, the precursors of breadboards, at the Hospital of St Cross. (See the 'Origins' section.) Established in the 1130s, St Cross offered the Wayfarer's Dole; a free hunk of bread and a horn of ale to travellers in need of sustenance. The victuals were presented on a round trencher with the characteristic cross of St Cross in silver inlay in the centre. It was generous and also judicious: it saved having itinerants and vagrants collapsing from exhaustion on their patch.

St Cross Round. The board is of ancient oak, which is not of good enough quality to make a robust board. The maker had to patch up structural cracks and a large nail hole on both sides, where the wood had gone black with the rust.

St Cross Round, silver inlay, 1800s, the reverse stamped 'D. Frost, The Square, Winchester', ancient oak, 13 ½ inches.

Cross of St Cross. St Cross adopted the blazon of the Knights of St John, The Hospitallers, in the 1160s, after funding them to establish the Hospital in Jerusalem and ensure safe passage to and from it. The 'Argent a cross potent between four plain crosslets or', was simplified leaving just the central cross, which resembles four 'T's joined at the foot. St Cross was founded by Henri de Blois in the Cluniac tradition, which prioritised giving help to travellers. And incredibly they still are! Visitors can enjoy the 'Wayfarers' Dole' for a modest sum.

King Alfred's College. Mr Austin Laverty was also Head of the Handicraft Department, which ground to a halt during the Second World War as the building was requisitioned. After being returned to civilian use, Mr Harris remembers organising a collection among the returning teachers to re-equip the school. From the money, he bought twelve breadboards from Mr Laverty 'beautifully carved with sheaves of corn' for the Refectory. 'One for each table.' A potent symbol of life returning to normal.

Fabric Fund. The Lavertys carved oak boards in prolific numbers, enough to contribute a whopping £2,000 to the restoration fund target of £85,000. Their souvenirs included dishes, crucifixes and bread trenchers and they ran a stall outside the Cathedral selling their goods, and a shop which closed in the 1950s.

'This is the Round Table of King Arthur'. Edwin Laverty made a name for himself carving miniaturised Round Tables in the form of breadboards, possibly

'This is the Round Table of King Arthur', Laverty, newly felled oak, circa 1950.

from 1915. The large replica dating from the 13th century hangs in Winchester Castle. The detail on the face of Arthur is impressive and the incised lettering very fine. Some of the Winchester boards are of oak that does not look or feel 1,000 years old. It is likely demand outstripped supply and the Winchester carvers sourced seasoned oak from elsewhere.

Presented to Royalty. Edwin Laverty was invited to make and present one 'carved in oak 500 years old', with legs, to Queen Elizabeth in 1955, 'for the Royal children'. His brother Austin presented one to Prince Charles in 1978, four years before the last of the eight brothers passed away.

Marks & Bramhall. While Laverty's worked with the Cathedral, and owned their own showrooms, other souvenir retailers sprang up such as Marks of Winchester. Marks asked Bramhall as early as the 1930s, to make their own version of Arthur's Round Table bread boards. A wide variety of products were available.

'Benedictus', 1926, newly felled oak, 16 ¾ x 11 inches.

'Benedictus'. Grace is carved in Latin around this board, '*Benedictus, Benedicat, Benedicto, Benedicatur*', translating as 'May the Blessed One give a Blessing', before dinner and 'Let the Blessed be Blessed' for after dinner. A silver plaque on the reverse reads, 'H & K, June 3, 1901-1926.'

'Ave Mater Angliae'. It appears Canterbury also had boards produced, this one showing the trademark 'C' of a Wing /Bramhall creation. Canterbury Cathedral shop is still offering 'Nave Roof Oak Pens', from oak felled in 1490 and turned in Britain. Proceeds go towards the 'Canterbury Journey' renovation project. Canterbury's motto: 'Hail Mother of England', refers to her status as Archbishopric, the head of the worldwide Anglican Communion. Famous Archbishops include St Augustine (the founder), Lanfranc, St Dunstan, St Anselm and Thomas à Beckett.

The 'Argent three choughs Proper' topped by a Royal Lion are the arms of Thomas à Beckett. The right-hand shield represents the diocese of Canterbury. Again, out of 121 archbishops, Thomas à Beckett has been singled out, possibly due to his murder on the orders of Henry II in 1170. By killing Thomas unarmed in the cathedral, the King's knights broke codes of chivalry and sanctity. Even in a harsh medieval world, it ranked as an atrocity never to be forgotten or repeated.

'Ave Mater Angliae', souvenir of Canterbury, Bramhall, circa 1935, oak, 12 inches.

Bread Knives and Forks

1. Ave Mater Angliae on ribbons, Canterbury motto, a bread fork to accompany the board, by Bramhall.
2. Manners Makyth Man on a ribbon, Gothic, with Winchester Cathedral arms, and thin wheat on back, boxwood, by Laverty.
3. Bramhall's Manners Makyth Man, square lettering on a ribbon, with flowers and foliage, to match a breadboard, oak, circa 1950s.

Bread knives and forks, Winchester and Canterbury, oak, steel and silver plate.

4. Winchester fork, topped with a Bishop's mitre, with leaves and wheat, oak and EPNS.

5-6. Large Manners Makyth Man handle, topped with a Bishops Mitre, the square lettering on a ribbon, the arms of William of Wykeham on the upper side, the Cathedral on the underside, early pieces carved by Laverty, oak.

Tom Samuel of London

Active today, Tom is a true artist in the bloodline of William Gibbs Rogers. No two of his creations are alike. He has a rule: if it hasn't been done before, then it's worth trying. His style is curvaceous and voluptuous, incorporating classical themes with an original twist. He has come to carve eight breadboards, rather by accident, thanks to his long association with Rosslyn.

Tom's version of events. 'During the 1990s, Rosslyn, as a dealer in breadboards, wanted to find a source for new breadboards. She visited Bramhall in Sheffield

Sycamore blank, turned, 14 inches.

Samuel's Swirligig, 1990s, sycamore, 13 inches.

and was also looking for more ornate boards of one piece of wood. She began to pressurise me to make some. My excuse was that I did not have suitable wood. She then arrived with some blanks.

'My next excuse was that they were too wet to use. She brought them back every time I saw her and we weighed them on our kitchen scales. After about a year their weight had stabilised so I had to have a go.

'What occurred to me is that once I had allowed enough of a surface to cut the bread on, I could do what I liked with everything else. Much as I love old breadboards, I wanted to do what had not been done before,

Samuel's Octopus, 2019, sycamore, 13 inches.

Samuel's Scrolls on a Roll, 2019, sycamore, 13 inches.

while at the same time echoing what was good about the old ones. What I like is creating an impression of movement and the feeling that they are alive. I did make four boards for her in the 1990s which I really enjoyed. Although the turning part is hard work, it is a short amount of time compared with the carving and shaping which is the fun part. The boards were experimental and all different. I gave them to her to sell, but they ended up part of the collection.

Samuel's Crumb-catcher, 2019, sycamore, 13 inches.

'When I was helping Madeleine curate and caption the collection, two more blanks appeared. So I made four more boards for Madeleine, two based on Vitruvian scrolls, the others with tapered reeds and receding beading. These are more refined than the first four, but I am pleased with them all and hear they get chosen to present the scones regularly at the museum.

'I have found more wood so who knows what I will do next. I hope others are inspired to have a go. The great thing is, this is such an unexplored area, it is very easy to be original. The making of them is not easily explained in a book, so we are planning to film a documentary! I hope to demonstrate to artists in wood the techniques I use.

'I refuse to cut corners. For example, the chuck is glued to the reverse of the breadboard, for mounting on the lathe, avoiding the use of nails and screws. As it is on excess wood, this must then be removed. This method preserves the integrity and strength of the wood where it will receive the most wear.'

The chuck on the reverse of a breadboard-to-be.

'Be Thankful', George Wing, 1860s-1920s, sycamore, 12 inches.

Our heartfelt thanks to Team BB

Tom Samuel, our Consultant, Artist in Wood, Carver and Cabinet-maker: "This whole adventure started when I needed some caning done. That is when I was working in furniture restoration in about 1986. I had four solid ivory chairs reputedly looted from Tipu Sultan's palace that needed new cane seats. These chairs and a table belonged to the Sir John Soane's Museum, I had put them back together from fragments that Peter Thornton and I found in every nook and cranny of the museum, they were remarkably near complete. I did not want them out of my sight, I had to find someone who would cane the seats in our workshop. I found an advertisement for 'Weaver Neave And Daughter' in the yellow pages and after some heavy persuasion Rosslyn Neave agreed to come and do them. She enjoyed coming to the workshop so much from then on she did all our caning there, she was liked especially for her amusing turn of phrase and was known as 'Miss Whiplash'.

"It soon became clear that she had a stall at Bermondsey and Portobello (to give the fingers a rest). This is when my education in breadboards and knives began.

"At first she was just a dealer but she began to get seller's remorse when she sold something she knew she would never see again and the idea of a collection and even a book began to emerge.

"When I gave up restoration full time and began a more creative and even less lucrative career, Rosslyn would come every few months and have lunch with my wife Anne and myself. She would show us all her latest discoveries and we discussed lines of research. Her interests were wide and it was difficult to keep her to the subject, so, many red herrings were followed.

"This went on for about twenty years. In that time I made a few breadboards for her and I realized that there was more to the subject than anybody would have expected. Her dementia began to show and we fell out over something silly.

"After Rosslyn's death I got a call from her daughter Madeleine asking for help sorting out Rosslyn's possessions. It was clear that something would have to be done about the ominous sag in her bedroom ceiling, this was caused by twenty four boxes of papers and about ten boxes of breadboards. We decided to edit the papers to only those that related to breadboards and knives which turned out to be three boxes. The story that emerged when the references were put in chronological order surprised me, in how little has changed.

"This snippet from 'Carving in Wood' in *The Art-Union* of 1833 pretty much nails it:

This beautiful and interesting art constituted formerly an independent vocation, and so received its share of direct patronage; but it is now...not generally recognised

259

as a branch of art requiring taste and unwearied application to attain to successful results…[I]t is highly desirable that a body [of men] so respectable, should have something beyond the wages of journeymen mechanics to look forward to…It is a subject of bitter complaint among them that the profits and credit of their best works are reaped either by upholsterers or dealers…An opportunity is now at hand [the building of the new Houses of Parliament] which must call them forth from the obscurity whence have issued for a long series of years their anonymous works… [and] afford them the opportunity of exhibiting the state of their art…We trust that better days are in store for them.

"What strikes me is how many breadboards and knives must have been made. The elaborate ones in good condition are very beautiful but even the plainest or most worn ones still have a charm. It is also a surprise that museum visitors still cherish their heirloom boards.

"This book has been in the pipeline for nearly twenty years, what held her back was wanting to write the definitive book on the subject. I hope it will lead to many new discoveries and a better awareness of this popular art form. I congratulate Madeleine and Catheryn for spreading the word."

Tom Samuel, Feb 2019.

Tom Samuel, Brother at the Art Workers' Guild, with his new breadboard, 'Scrolls on a roll', 2018. His name is up on the wall behind.

Kourosh Monirzad, our fine art photographer, Unica Art Services:
"It was a painstaking process, just setting up the equipment in the tiny house, already chock-solid with the collection, excess furniture and curios. It all had to be cleared to one end of the room, and put back meticulously at the end, because Rosslyn was not to know that her daughter was trying to manage things.

"We came on Saturdays when Rosslyn would be at Portobello, too frail to do a whole day, too muddled to give the correct change, too scatty to keep her handbag safe. Surreptitiously we were making a record of her life's work, in case she gave them away to a hawker, or burnt the house down leaving the hob on.

"We chose a fine art look with soft multi-directional lighting to raise the carving from all angles. Glare was a challenge on the highly polished items, the porcelain and silver-plate. Patiently we ploughed through them one by one, with various exposures, retaking if necessary.

"One day Madeleine showed me the Katrin Cargill photo dating from 2009. 'You could do that in here,' I said. So I jumped on a chair and mounted nine boards on the chimney breast in the front room as an experiment, to replicate the magazine interior. They looked so impressive suddenly, all the oak ones together. That showed Madeleine how to get them off the floor and paved the way for the gallery later on.

"My work as a fine art gallery manager gave me access to many skilled restorers whose details I shared, so that the contents of the house which were mostly damaged, could be made useable again for the family. Steve Crittenden hung them carefully, so they were all even and equidistant, the deeply carved ones higher up, the similar wood tones grouped. He also made special brackets for the knives to hang safely. I advised on lighting and tracking, wall colour and the arrangement of the furniture.

"I am glad to have helped Madeleine over numerous obstacles on this often painful journey, and am proud to see my photos so beautifully displayed in this book. The deal is: when she has made a million, I'll take 10%!"

Kourosh Monirzad, 2019

Marie Lester, our recipe maker, baker and stylist:
"In January 2016, I was struck a devastating blow: the loss of my mother. Nothing had prepared me emotionally for this life-changing event.

"In the months and years that followed, I found myself wanting to bake. I had always been a keen cook but this was different. I wanted to make pastry and pies and cakes and breads. Later I read that smell and touch are the two key senses involved with strong feelings of nostalgia. My mother had baked every day when my brothers and I were children. There were always wonderful apple pies, crumbles, treacle puddings, cakes galore – and our favourite butterscotch meringue pie! And now I was filling my kitchen and home with those evocative aromas of culinary alchemy.

ACKNOWLEDGEMENTS

"What was left of my mother's baking equipment was still in my parents' house at that point, being used primarily by myself when I stayed with my father. The wooden breadboard and bread knife that I had grown up with, always on the table in the living room, were long since lost. As was my mother's old cane mixing bowl. So, to compensate, I set about collecting Victorian and Edwardian kitchenalia: mixing bowls, rolling pins, pastry boards, bread knives, butter dishes – and breadboards.

"The different colours and textures of "treen", the term given to small wooden items, began to fascinate me. Wooden tools are wonderfully tactile to use. And breadboards, in particular, were compelling. The wood colour, the sizes, the variety of carvings: hops, flowers, acorns, wheat… The wheatsheaf symbol became another magnet and again, reading about this later, I found to my surprise that it was a symbol of mourning in the Victorian period.

Marie Lester, 2019

"In the course of my collecting, I came across a lady in nearby Putney who had recently inherited from her mother a whole host of breadboards and knives. I also discovered that she had created a museum – in her home – which one could visit. The idea of learning about the history and designs of breadboards over a cup of tea and a scone was very appealing so off I went.

"And so I met Madeleine.

"I visited her a couple of times and we ended up talking about the book she was about to write. She mentioned that it was to contain some recipes, and to my delight she said 'you've got the job'.

"It has been great fun working with Madeleine. It turns out that we share a similar sense of humour, and enjoy the creative side of pairing recipes with boards and photographing the various cakes and loaves we have chosen for the 'Recipes' section. And of course, devouring them over a lovely cup of tea!

"The recipes selected are mostly traditional. Above all, they are easy to make, very tasty and visually appealing."

Marie Lester, April 2019

Martin Fletcher, our forester:

"We come from the woods. Our monkey minds feel at home in forests, tree houses, log cabins and saunas. Look at our childish joy at the must-have stick, the lean-to den, camp-fires and tree-climbing. We may have progressed to concrete and steel and yet love holidaying in natural surroundings to recharge and relax.

Martin giving me a lecture on wood, 2019.

"Wood was also key to our survival and our livelihood; the giving tree provided food, warmth and shelter in a harsh, dangerous world. Mesolithic man was already making wood into tools and utensils to keep food off the floor, no doubt.

"Wood may be less durable, but isn't that ideal? It doesn't create refuse mountains or poisonous water. And contrary to common misconceptions, if forests are well managed, here is so much wood out there, ready for the felling. An interesting fact: during your average two-hour walk in a large wood, the trees might have cumulatively grown a tonne of new wood, right above your very head! They are growing whilst you are sleeping.

"The joy of a breadboard is that it brings the soothing effect of wood into our busy lives, in a useful and decorative way. Every time we need a slice of bread, it is at the ready, becoming inextricably linked with feeling full, safe and loved.

"Sycamore was an excellent choice of wood because it grows well in many parts of this country, particularly in the middle and north of England and can stand the climate there better than beech and is mature within eighty years. Also, it has a regular, close grain and does not splinter. It was used traditionally for utensils coming into contact with food such as butter moulds, chopping boards and draining boards, as, crucially, it does not "taste", nor go furry when scrubbed and happens to be a clean-looking colour.

"This collection is fascinating as I can also tell the story of the tree which the breadboard was made from. For example, in one oak board, there are very marked differences in the patterning of the grain. In one part, the growth rings are tight together, meaning the tree was distressed for years. While in another part, the rings are wide apart, showing the tree was burgeoning. This suggests the location became better managed, with more light for crown development.

"Oak is not an immediate choice for food-related utensils as the grain is wide and moisture gets trapped, causing swelling. It is also heavier to handle and not so easy to carve as the grain is more stubborn. But there are a number of interesting Winchester boards of oak which were a pleasure to handle. One board mentions the wood came from the old cathedral, built by William the Conqueror in 1086. For an oak tree to be large enough for a nave roof beam, it would have to be about 200 years old and would thus have been a sapling in the early 900's A.D.

"It has been a pleasure advising Madeleine about her collection, identifying the tree-lets in her 'Pinetum', aka the garden, overseeing care of the Council's young trees in her street and taking her on a visit of the New Forest where woodland dating back to the Ice Age can still be enjoyed."

Martin Fletcher, 2019

General Acknowledgements

Our hundreds of visitors and followers for sharing their enthusiasm and anecdotes.
Marty Free for decorating, hanging the tracking and spot lights.
Sarah and Andy Parkinson of Meedja for attractive WAF fliers and greetings cards.
Frances Allitt at *The Antiques Trade Gazette* for a 'Dealer's Diary' write-up.
Julia Bright of Wandsworth Community Radio for a podcast with Rosslyn.
Stephanie Hartman, *Time Out,* for article on our museum, part of their all-new Boring London section (tsk!).
Chris Evans, *Daily Telegraph,* for publishing our reassuring letter about Bath Abbey's pews.
Huon Mallalieu, *The Times,* for a feature on Collecting; and County Life Museums feature.
Sir Peter Bazalgette, Chairman of the Arts Council, for making a great suggestion about galleries running B&Bs in 2016, which planted a seed.
Airbnb Experiences for endorsing the Museum Tour.
Katt Adachi, MA in Journalism at the University of Westminster, for a museum podcast.
Kyle ap Simon, Octopus Books, for including us in Richard Bertinet's book *Crumb.*
Jean Cazals for photographing our boards so beautifully.
Cath Mattos, at Wandsworth Arts Fringe, for being open-minded enough to give us an airing.
Joan Ransley for posting an attractive shot of the museum on her 'insta' site after a visit.
JP Devlin, *Saturday Live,* BBC R4, for an exceptional field trip to the BB Museum.
Jason Rosam, BBC Radio London, for an interview about collecting.

Anthony Bailey, *Woodworking Crafts Magazine,* for a lush 4-page museum article.
Georgina Wroe, *Antique Collectors' Magazine,* for another lush Collector's Guide write up.
Ruth Marler for local newspaper searches which threw up fascinating insights.
Dani Meyer for advising about the book, with cover designs and chapters.
Sara Basquill, Lincolnshire Archives, for permitting use of a photo for an affordable sum.
Emma Kay, Food Historian, for generously putting me in touch with Prospect Books.
Catheryn Kilgarriff, Prospect Books, for taking a chance on us!
Brendan King, for meticulously and patiently massaging my hotchpotch of materials into this smooth reading, visually appealing book.
Jane for inviting us to be part of their silent auctions for The Compassionate Friends.
And Jane for another silent auction for Our Lady of Victories Primary School.
And Antonia Wainman, another for Lady Margaret's School, Fulham.
Elizabeth Lynch for inviting us to the What's Next Wandsworth group meetings
Sara O'Donnell at Enable Wandsworth, the culture branch of Wandsworth Council, for selecting us for the Culture Map.
Chris Gray of the Bakehouse, Putney, for selling our boards and stocking fliers
Ray, Hurlingham Books, for clearing the house of books so we could start the refurb, and displaying our flier in his window.
Charlene Coleman, Putney Library, for inviting us to exhibit and do the first 'Talk and Cheese'.
Bernie Love, Genesis Imaging, for great framed photos for our Putney Library exhibition.
Victoria Garthwaite, Friends of Putney School of Arts, for offering us a table at their Christmas fair.
Christopher Scott, The Worshipful Company of Turners, for offering us a table at their fair.
Ernie Rubinstein, Ph.D., Associate Librarian Emeritus, Drew University, for translating the Jewish motto and being unstintingly encouraging.
Marie-Isabelle de Gendre, INALCO, Université de Paris IX, for translating the Russian mottos.
Victoria Tam, Hong Kong University, for translating and analysing the Chinese motto.
Jennifer Hollingdale, textile artist and printmaker, for having fun with her board.
Clive Nash, Woodentops Woodcarving Club, for giving us a rapturous write-up.
Paul Freeman, for photographing some items beautifully for Rosslyn early on.
Avril Horsford, Putney WI, for inviting the Antique Breadboard Museum to be part of their lecture programme.
Ghaith Somai, Vistaprint, for getting the flier right, no squeaking, no charge
Natasha Hume, for welcoming the boards to embellish St Margaret's Harvest Lunch.

Br. Stephen Fowler, *Fortean Times*, for labelling us Officially Quirky as of January 2019.

Deborah Taylor and Debbie Hawkesbury, author's advice, freely and generously given.

Hugh Wedderburn, Master Carvers' Association, for introductions, networking and events.

Daniel Carpenter and Emma, Heritage Crafts Association, for sending out a call for carvers.

Liz Nicholls, Round and About Putney, for running a Christmas spot.

Marina Sacco, Local Roots, BAC, for organising a training day for creatives in business.

Judith Chegwidden, Putney Society, for mentioning the Antique Breadboard Museum in their newsletter.

Nic McElhatton, Consultant, Christies, for sharing his knowledge on treen, and for writing the Foreword.

Neil Adams, Borthwick Institute, York, for super efficient and affordable archiving.

Anne Samuel for proof-reading everything.

Frank Hastings in 2003 for sending anecdotes and 'Century's Progress Yorkshire' of 1893.

Mark Pattinson for showing me around the Somerset Rural Life Museum where we found a Jubilee board.

Michael Ford and Sam Rayne, National Trust Devon, for their assistance with the Saltram board.

David Haynes and his descendants for sharing the Bramhall archives and collection.

Terence Whewell, MD, Bramhall 1840, for allowing Rosslyn to photograph the Wing heritage boards.

The Townswomen's Guild, for another talk.

Great Dunmow History Society, and another.

Kate Kern at Fulham Palace for welcoming the boards to their family fun craft day 'Designed by Dunstan'.

Catherine Lock, *The New Craftsmen*, for nominating us 'Best London Discovery' in *Homes & Gardens*.

Sarah Holloway and The Heritage Open day team at the National Trust for organising this great national event of free culture.

Emma Anthony at GLL/BETTER for including us in their Wandsworth Heritage Programme.

Helen Ainsworth for performing her show 'Janet' in the gallery.

Isadora Vibes for performing her show 'Soak' in our bathroom!

Cat Parkinson at Airbnb for coordinating the *Metro* article 'My Odd Job'.

Josh Munns at the Breast Cancer Haven in Fulham for recognising our 'Big Tea Cosy' contribution.

Silvia Macchia, editor at *Parish*, the magazine for St Mary's Church, Putney, for offering a double spread, beautifully laid out.

Catherine O'Keeffe at the Art Workers' Guild for inviting us to their Table Top Museum event as part of a London Open House event. And again for 'The Art of Making' exhibition as part of London Craft Week.

Lucie Neame at Oak and Rope, for sending a lovely sample of their work engraved with 'An Antique breadboard of the future'.

Robert Dex, *Evening Standard*, for giving us headline status alongside sex toys.

Maggie Tyson, Local Studies Librarian at Sheffield City Archives, for publishing their entire Wing catalogue online at www.picturesheffield.com, and for promising to buy the book! (That's one in the bag then, Catheryn.)

Brian and Elizabeth Stratton, for including us in their walking guide, *12 Bridges London*.

Bill Nash, for submitting to a cream tea and tour as the price to pay for including us in their updated 'Secret London' guide book.

Sue and Mike Witts of Appleby Antiques for sharing their hard-earned knowledge.

Mikki Towler of The Antique Kitchen for contributing a photo to the Wing section.

Richard, Lester, Sue and Mike, and all the other dealers who ran the boards to her over the years.

Joyce Stephenson and the descendants of William Gibbs Rogers for sharing heirlooms.

And finally my family, who were coerced into helping:

Tadashi, for taste-testing the best of Putney's scones and jam, and ferreting out documents.

Nicholas, for IT and social media skills, designing the blog, advising on layout.

Emily, for taking the 'weird but wonderful' approach to home life.

Picture acknowledgements

Photograph of Rosslyn Neave on page 2, Antique Breadboard Museum Archives.

Photograph of Wing breadboard on title page courtesy of Paul Freeman.

Photograph on page 3 courtesy of Nic McElhatton.

Photograph of Madeleine Neave on page 8, courtesy of Jerry Syder for Metro.co.uk.

Photographs of Portobello Market Stall on page 14, and composite moulding on page 69 by Madeleine Neave.

Bibliography

— *A Catalogue of English Art Manufactures: Selected for their Beauty of Design* (London: Addey and Co., 1853).

—*The Century's Progress: Yorkshire* (London: London Printing and Engraving Co, 1893).

—*The City of Winchester Directory and Illustrated Almanac for 1877* (Winchester: Tanner & Sons, 1877).

— *The Illustrated Exhibitor: A Tribute to the World's Industrial Jubilee* (London: Cassell, 1851).

Army and Navy Co-operative Society. *Yesterday's Shopping: The Army & Navy Stores Catalogue, 1907* (London: David & Charles, 1969).

Beeton, Isabella. *Beeton's Book of Household Management* (London: Beeton Publishing, 1861).

Benham, William. *Winchester: Diocesan Histories* (London: SPCK, 1884).

Benson, Peter. *Whittling Handbook* (London: Guild of Master Craftsman Publications, 2016).

Biddle, Martin & Beatrice Clayre. *Winchester Castle and the Great Hall* (Hampshire: Hampshire County Council, 1983).

Cleve, Clifton. *The Book of Inventions* (London: Henry Hurst, 1848).

Cole, Henry. *Fifty years of public work of Sir Henry Cole, K.C.B., accounted for in his deeds, speeches and writings* (London: G. Bell, 1884).

Collins, Michael. *The Likes of Us: An Official Biography of the White Working Class* (London: Granta Books, 2004).

Day, Ivan. *Eat Drink and Be Merry* (London: Philip Wilson Ltd, 2000).

Flook, Ron. *The London Knife Book, An A-Z Guide to London Cutlers 1820-1945* (Antique Knives Ltd, 2008).

Hollister-Short, Graham (ed). *History of Technology*, Volume 20, The Institute of Historical Research, University of London (London: A&C Black, 1998).

Hope, Douglas George. *Thomas Arthur Leonard and the Co-operative Holidays Association* (Newcastle-Upon-Tyne: Cambridge Scholars Publishing, 2017).

Hopewell, Peter. *Saint Cross: England's Oldest Almshouse* (Phillimore & Co, 1995).

Humbert, Lewis Macnaughten. *Memorials of the Hospital of Saint Cross and Alms House of Noble Poverty* (London: Parker & Co, 1868).

Kirby, T.F. *Annals of Winchester College: From its Foundation in the Year 1382 to the Present Time* (London: Kessinger, 2010).

Lower, Mark Antony, *The Worthies of Sussex* (Lewes: Printed For Subscribers Only, 1865).

Mayhew, Henry. *London Labour and the London Poor* (London: Charles Griffin & Co, 1864).

National Art Library. *A List of Works Illustrating Sculpture in the National Art Library* (London: Eyre & Spottiswode, 1886).

Neale, J. P. *Views of the Seats, Mansions, Castle etc. of Noblemen and Gentlemen in England, Wales Scotland and Ireland* (London: Jones, c.1829).

Pater, Stephan. *Der Schatzbehalter oder Schrein der waren reichtümer des heils unnd ewyger seligkeit* (Nuremberg: Anton Koberger, circa 1445-1513).

Raistrick, Arthur (ed.). *The Century's Progress: Yorkshire Industry and Commerce* (Brenton Publishing, 1971).

Roberts, Howell. *Dr Thomas Richard Allinson* (Maidenhead: Allinson, 1973)

Rogers, George Arthur. *The Art of Woodcarving* (London: Virtue & Co, 1867).

—*Some Account of the Woodcarvings of St Michael's Church, Cornhill* (London: George Berridge, 1867).

Rogers, William Gibbs. *List of Carvings and Other Works of Art* (London, 1854).

Smith, H. Clifford. *Catalogue of English Furniture & Woodwork. Vol. I. Gothic and Early Tudor* (London: Board of Education, 1929).

Stevens, Charles. *Winchester Notions: The English Dialect of Winchester* College (London: Athlone Press, 1998).

Stephenson, Joyce A. *The Wood Carvings by William Gibbs Rogers for St. Michael's Church Cornhill* (Published by the author, 2009).

Swift, Jonathan. *A Tale of a Tub* (London: Penguin, 2004).

Tweedale, Geoffrey. *The Sheffield Knife Book, A History and Collector's Guide* (Sheffield: Hallamshire Press, 1996).

Victoria & Albert Museum. *Catalogue: Exhibition of Victorian and Edwardian Decorative Arts* (London: Her Majesty's Stationery Office, 1952).

Wallis T. W. *Autobiography of Thomas Wilkinson Wallis, Sculptor in Wood, and Extracts from his Sixty Years' Journal with Twenty-four Illustrations and Four Diagrams* (Louth: J.W. Goulding & Son, 1899).

Waring, John Burley. *Masterpieces of Industrial Art & Sculpture at the International Exhibition 1862* (London: Day & Co, 1863).

Welch, Charles. *History of the Cutlers' Company of London* (London: Cutlers' Company, 1916).

Wesley, John. *Minutes of the Methodist Conferences* (London: Wesleyan Conference Office, 1874)

Whorton, James C. *Inner Hygiene: Constipation and the Pursuit of Health in Modern Society* (Oxford University Press, 2000).

Wing, George. *Catalogue of Wooden Goods* (Sheffield, 1887). Original at Sheffield Local Studies Library (674.8 SSTQ).

Worde, Wynkyn de. *The Boke of Keruynge* (London, 1508).

Periodicals

The Art-Union
Belfast Telegraph
The Great North Magazine
Hampshire Chronicle
Homes & Gardens
Illustrated London News
Manchester Evening News
Punch
The Scotsman
The Sheffield Telegraph
The Sheffield Star
Somerset Herald

Websites

The Aesthetic Sense (www.theaestheticsense.com). Artisanal website.
The Antique Kitchen (www.theantiquekitchen.co.uk). Antique pine furniture and kitchenalia.
Ancestry.Com (www.ancestry.com). For genealogical research.
Ancestry Images (www.ancestryimages.com). Free image archive.
The Collecting Bug (www.thecollectingbug.com).
Encyclopedia Britannica (www.britannica.com).

Greater Manchester 1914 (GM1914wordpress.com). The First World War in Manchester.

Internet Archive (www.archive.org). A library of free books and other online media sources.

Joyce Stephenson (woodcarverschildren.weebly.com). About William Gibbs Rogers and his descendants.

Lurgan Ancestry (www.lurganancestry.com). Documenting the history of the Lurgan area.

My Wesleyan Methodists (www.mywesleyanmethodists.org.uk). Research website devoted to every aspect of Wesleyan Methodist history.

Public Records Office (www.nationalarchives.gov.uk). Database and archives of the Public Records Office.

Sheffield Indexers (www.sheffieldindexers.com). Local history site and database.

Sheffield City Archives & Local Studies Library (www.sheffield.gov.uk). Local history site.

Swedish Wood (www.swedishwood.com). Information about wood.

University of Glasgow History of Art and HATII online database (www.sculpture.gla.ac.uk). Mapping the Practice and Profession of Sculpture in Britain and Ireland 1851-1951.

Wikipedia (www.wikipedia.com). General reference.

Wolverhampton History & Heritage Website (www.historywebsite.co.uk). Archive material relating to Wolverhampton.